Flood, Patricia,
author.

Susan Benson

D1737923

DISCARD

SUSAN BENSON

SUSAN BENSON

Art, Design and Craft on Stage

Patricia Flood

FIREFLY BOOKS

A FIREFLY BOOK

Published by Firefly Books Ltd. 2019
Copyright © 2019 Firefly Books Ltd.
Text copyright © Patricia Flood 2019
Photographs © as listed on page 140

First printing

Library of Congress Control Number: 2018957840

Library and Archives Canada Cataloguing in Publication
Flood, Patricia, author
        Susan Benson : art, design and craft on stage / by Patricia Flood.

Includes bibliographical references and index.
ISBN 978-0-228-10177-2 (hardcover)

        1. Benson, Susan. 2. Set designers--Canada--Biography.
3. Theaters--Stage-setting and scenery. 4. Biographies. I. Title.

PN2096.B46F66 2019   792.02'5092   C2018-905393-3

Published in the United States by
Firefly Books (U.S.) Inc.
P.O. Box 1338, Ellicott Station
Buffalo, New York 14205

Published in Canada by
Firefly Books Ltd.
50 Staples Avenue, Unit 1
Richmond Hill, Ontario L4B 0A7

Cover and interior design by Scott McKowen and Allysha Witt
Copy Editor, Kathryn Harvey; Firefly Copy Editor, Dan Liebman

Printed in China

Canada We acknowledge the financial support of the Government of Canada.

The author is grateful for the support of the following, who made writing the book possible.

Contents

Design for the Queen of
the Night in *The Magic
Flute*, Minnesota Opera/
Dallas Opera, 1997.

Introduction

The initial impetus for this book was as a celebration of the career of a designer, teacher and mentor who is widely recognized as having a major influence on Canadian theatrical design over the past forty-plus years. It was also inspired by a need to preserve an important part of this history. I first met Susan Benson when she was Head of Design at the Stratford Festival in the 1980s and I was a young assistant designer. We have kept in touch over the years, and the idea for this book evolved slowly as time passed.

One of the challenges of this project was to shed light on Susan Benson's creative process. She is very much an artist who chooses the theatre as her medium of expression. Many books on theatre design acknowledge some kind of creative, collaborative process as part of a designer's work but tend to focus on the technical perspective involved in the realization of a design. This would be an easy trap to fall into with Susan as her work with colour and texture, particularly in costume design, is unique and fascinating to write about. However, I also wanted to focus on the research, consultation and inspiration that lead up to a final design. This work, completed prior to any technical intervention, illustrates how her creative input plays an important dramaturgical role in the shaping of a production.

I also wanted to look at the crucial link between the creative and technical in the production of a piece of theatre and recognize the invaluable contribution of the many talented technicians and fellow artists who have helped bring Susan's work to the stage. It's impossible for her to talk about a show she's designed without mentioning the tremendous support and appreciation she has for the many people who have brought her designs to life on the stage. One of the great pleasures of researching this book has been the conversations I have had with many theatre technicians and fellow artists who have worked with her and have great respect for her work.

Finally, without getting up on too big of a soapbox, I feel it is vital that we honour and preserve our theatre tradition and the creative people in it. Susan Benson has been a leader, teacher and mentor to hundreds of people either directly or indirectly, and that contribution needs to be recognized. I want to emphasize the valuable resources that theatre archives provide: in particular, the LW Conolly Theatre Archives at the University of Guelph, the archives at Theatre Museum Canada, the Stratford Festival, the National Ballet of Canada and the Canadian Opera Company. This book would not be possible without their help and the access they have given me to their collections. They are preserving a vital part of our artistic history.

This book has been written from Susan Benson's own notes and archival material as well as from my knowledge, direct experience and conversations with Susan over the many years of our friendship. Although the words are my own, I have tried, as much as possible, to be true to Susan's voice and perspective.

PATRICIA FLOOD

A BRIEF BIOGRAPHY

Susan Benson has played a major role in the development of Canadian theatre, opera and ballet over the past forty years. Her work with theatres across Canada, the United States, Australia, Europe and China is a reflection of excellence in theatrical production.

Born and educated in Great Britain, she worked at the Royal Shakespeare Company and the BBC before she came to Canada in 1966. Since that time, she has collaborated with a wide range of internationally known actors, directors and choreographers at many theatres across Canada, including the Banff Centre, the Stratford Festival, the Canadian Opera Company and the National Ballet of Canada. Designs for theatre in the USA have included productions for the Arena Stage in Washington DC, the Denver Theatre Centre, the Guthrie Theatre, San Francisco and New York City Operas, the Opera Theatre of St. Louis and the Dallas Theatre Centre.

In addition to her eight Dora Mavor Moore awards,[1] she is an honorary member of the Associated Designers of Canada and has received a lifetime achievement award from the Canadian Association of Theatre Technology, the Paul D. Fleck Fellowhship from the Banff Centre plus the Banff Centre Award for contributions to the Arts in Canada and a Canadian Actor's Equity Honorary Membership for Contributions to Canadian Theatre. With her husband, lighting designer Michael J. Whitfield, she was part of the formation of the Associated Designers of Canada in the 1970s. She has taught at the National Theatre School of Canada, the Banff Centre, Carnegie Mellon University and the University of Illinois.

Her theatre work has been exhibited in many venues including the Lincoln Centre in New York as part of their exhibition, *Women Designers of the 20th Century*. She is included in the Canadian and International editions of Who's Who of Women and is a member of the Royal Canadian Academy of Arts. She continues to work actively as a painter from her studio in Salt Spring Island, British Columbia.

A complete chronology of her theatre design work is included on pages 130 to 137.

The Making of a Designer

Benson's maternal grandmother (stage name Barbara Verne) seated on the left with a shawl over her shoulders, on tour in the west of England, early 1920s.

Design for Lucy Peacock as Marie in *Blessings in Disguise*. Manitoba Theatre Centre, Winnipeg, 1998. Opposite: Barbara Verne (Benson's grandmother) in *The Little Dutch Girl* (*Das Hollandweibchen*) in London's West End, 1920.

THE EARLY YEARS

Susan Benson was born in Bexley Heath, Kent, in 1942, one of two children from a family with a great love for the theatre. Her father wrote many comedy scripts for the BBC as well as scripts for well-known British comedians such as Charlie Chester, Arthur English and Avril Angers, and her grandmother was an actress who worked with well-known actors of the day. Her mother, a director and writer, ran a theatre school and coached aspiring artists auditioning to enter major schools in Britain such as LAMDA (The London Academy of Music and Dramatic Art) and RADA (The Royal Academy of Dramatic Art). At this school, Benson trained as an actress, studying character development, stage movement, period movement and voice. This understanding of how an actor works was essential to her later career as a designer.

She was taken to the theatre at a very young age and her appreciation of the visual power of theatre started when she saw a variety show with different comedy sketches featuring the Crazy Gang with Nervo and Knox, a popular British comedy troupe of the 1940s and '50s. In her own words:

> I remember laughing at a running gag of one of the Crazy Gang following a girl with a grass skirt across the stage with a lawn mower. Each time she appeared, followed by the lawn mower, her grass skirt would get shorter. Even though I was quite young, I got the gag and thought it was very funny. I was also taken with a set of showgirls dressed in very brief space costumes covered in a silver fabric. I was only about four or five years old but still have the program and the photograph of these particular 1940s outfits which now look very dated. (Benson interview)

Liberated from the restraints of World War Two, British theatre was thriving and Benson's mother took her to a wide variety of productions in and around London. She also had a great aunt and uncle who lived in Stratford-upon-Avon and from the time she was fourteen, she would visit them and queue up outside the theatre at 4AM to get cheap tickets to see productions by the Royal Shakespeare Company. Here she saw a wonderful world of life, colour and imagination that inspired her. She was attracted to the idea of becoming a theatre designer from the time she was eight or nine years old. Although it was hard to give up acting, she chose design as she had always wanted to be an artist and designing allowed her to combine her love of painting and the theatre. She was aware of the work of well-known British designers like Tanya Moiseiwitsch and Lila De Nobili[1] and realized that women could work in this profession and be successful. She was supported in this career choice by her parents, whose encouragement made a great difference to success in later life.

Theatre offers a wonderful world of imagination and creativity to anyone seeking to explore new ways of seeing and making a difference in society, but it is also a cruel taskmaster. The hours are long; there is little money to be made;

and working conditions can border on the primitive. There are sometimes disappointments as struggling to create a successful piece of theatre can be extremely difficult. Those who choose this profession must have determination and tenacity combined with a great love for the work. Benson credits the support she received from her family as the solid and stable base she needed to believe in herself and her abilities. This love and support has carried her through the years.

The innovative design collaborative, Motley, say this in the preface to their book, *Designing and Making Stage Costumes*:

> Designing is an exacting profession. We do not recommend it for the faint-hearted or the indolent, and we presume that those who read the following pages will be neither. In them we will explain the methods and techniques that we have found advantageous, although the success of the aspirant designer must ultimately depend on his own ingenuity, and his capacity for hard work, originality and talent. We believe that the effort can be in some ways even more rewarding than the work of the creative painter. After all, even Botticelli never saw the beautiful clothes he painted come alive, worn by the finest performing talents of the age. (14)

A DEEPER UNDERSTANDING

Susan Benson's upbringing was especially fortunate as she began her artistic studies with a firm understanding and love for the theatre. She grew up in Great Britain, where theatre was a constant influence, an essential element of life and part of the social fabric of the time. For Benson, theatre is the stuff of life itself, appealing to all levels of the society it reflects. It is a place of happiness, fulfillment and the sharing of common goals. It is a welcoming place where people meet and communicate face to face and above all, it is a place of imagination. Imagination and creativity help with problem solving and enhance life in many ways. She feels that a healthy imagination is essential to the development of any human being and is vital to a full and compassionate life.

Benson's early experience acting and her love of art made her a natural for theatre design. Her first design, at the age of twelve, was for an adaptation of *Alice Through the Looking Glass* written by her mother and produced at her theatre school. At the age of fifteen, she began formal art training and this led to a decision, at the age of nineteen, to give up acting. She chose to study painting at Art College rather than the formal theatre design programs offered within the English College system; she knew that many well-known theatre designers at that time had come from a background of fine art. At Art College, Benson was able to augment her visual arts training with courses in different aspects of dress design, the history of costume, millinery and fabric printing. None of these studies were in any detail but touching on them helped her to understand processes that would be essential in her later career.

Benson trained primarily as a painter until she was in her early twenties. She attended several different schools over this period and believes this exposed her to diverse approaches to painting and helped her to develop her own uniquely independent style. This ability to understand a variety of artistic forms also enabled her to be more open to various styles and interpretations in response to different plays and historic periods. The choice to train as a painter meant Benson always thought of herself as a fine artist who chose theatrical design as an outlet for her creativity. It also gave her a firm foundation in the skills that would sustain her throughout her career. As she states,

> At the Wolverhampton College of Art, the Head of the Painting program really made us take time to look at shape, line, colour, proportion and rhythm. We had long, wonderful life drawing and painting sessions — really looking and understanding the body, becoming aware of the subtleties of colour and shape. This was so useful later in fittings ... really seeing what was there. (Benson interview)

Clockwise from top left: Jane Benson (Susan's mother) as Lady Britomart in *Major Barbara*, 1958; Susan with a fellow acting student in *The Rivals* at Attingham Park near Shrewsbury, 1960; Susan, age eighteen, in *Ring Round the Moon* while still at Art College; Susan as a young designer at the Krannert Centre, University of Illinois, 1970.

She not only learned the technical skills necessary to create beautiful set and costume renderings but also acquired the ability to see form, line, colour and proportion — essential for any designer. Both costume and set design are sculptural disciplines: the costumed actor, moving through a three-dimensional stage space, brings the play to life. Form, line, colour and proportion are manipulated by the designer in response to the script and are the basis of any design.

After completing her major program of study, Benson decided to take a final year at what was then the West of England College of Art. During this year, the students in the program were encouraged to study areas of the arts that they had not explored before. In her case, she decided to take some classes in contemporary machine embroidery and was also able to observe the couturier-level courses offered in bead embroidery. These classes showed her how fabric could be manipulated to create texture through appliqué, beading and embroidery, which greatly influenced her later approach to costume design. Here she saw the potential for fabric treatment and manipulation that has become a signature of her work.

Upon graduation from Art College, Benson wrote to Emma Selby Walker, who was in charge of the wardrobe at the Royal Shakespeare Company in Stratford-upon-Avon and was offered a position as a seamstress and general "dogsbody." This experience proved invaluable as she learned so much from observing what was happening in the wardrobe and backstage. During the production of *The Wars of the Roses* in 1963, designed by John Bury,[2] she was introduced to techniques for recreating historical clothing and armour. She saw that costumes were not just unembellished cloth cut out and sewn together, but that a lot of fabric treatment, such as dyeing and texturing, went into reimagining them in a more heightened, theatrical way. Through a variety of techniques, theatrical versions of period fabric were created with enhanced depth and dimension when seen from the distance of the stage.

Benson also learned many practical lessons such as how heavy a period costume can become and how difficult this can be for an actor. She once met Donald Sinden, a well-known senior actor in the company, coming up to the armoury to cut some metal pieces off his costume because he found it too heavy. Weight was something she had dealt with carrying some of the cloaks to backstage from the wardrobe across the road from the theatre. The realization may not seem that significant, but these early lessons informed her approach to costuming in later years.

Later experience working at the BBC in London in 1965 as a dresser again proved invaluable to her knowledge of the backstage world of the theatre. Here she worked on a wide variety of demanding shows with many renowned performers of the time. From the professional dressers who taught her, she learned innumerable backstage tips such as how to lace up a corset properly and what an opera singer looks for in a costume. On a large variety show requiring numerous changes, she learned how to arrange costume pieces properly for a quick change and how costume construction could help facilitate these changes. This knowledge later helped her work on *A History of American Film* for the National Arts Centre in Ottawa in 1980. The production required many rapid costume changes and influenced the way the costumes were designed. Benson was grateful to those early years at the BBC as she learned not only technique, but also organizational skills and an attitude of professionalism and responsibility that can be gained only through hands-on experience — something that cannot be underestimated.

COMING TO CANADA

Susan Benson's work at the BBC concluded when, in the early 1960s, her family immigrated to Vancouver, Canada, and her formal career as a theatre designer began. Benson found herself in a new country that was just finding itself theatrically. After many years of both British and American dominance, Canadian writers and producers were focused on finding a uniquely Canadian voice. It was a time of great support for the arts in Canada, and many small theatre companies sprang up as a result of federal and provincial grants. The heritage of British theatre made a significant contribution to Canadian culture, but the 1960s was a turning point. At this time, the cultural traditions of other immigrants to Canada and our own Indigenous peoples were beginning to be acknowledged as essential components of a new Canadian reality, and theatre reflected these values. This set of circumstances in her new home made finding work somewhat difficult for Benson. Whereas a designer with a British background and training would have been welcomed with open arms even a few years before, she would sometimes encounter a bias that favoured Canadian-born talent.

Despite this setback, Benson persevered, and eventually she was able to connect with many young directors working in small companies. This was an exciting, creative time for her as she was young, with no fear of failure and was able to be truly experimental

Designs for *Another Macbeth* and photo of Lady Macbeth, Krannert Center, University of Illinois, 1971.

in her work while honing her craft. She was also fortunate to be hired as an assistant costume designer at the Vancouver Playhouse under artistic director Malcolm Black. Her first production in Canada was an experimental theatre production for the Vancouver Playhouse Stage II, where she continued to design between 1966 and 1968.

At this time, Benson made two very important contacts that were instrumental in her future career. In 1966, she met Peter Franklin White, once a principal character dancer with the Royal Ballet in London who subsequently went to work as a movement coach at the University of Illinois. He recommended Benson to John Burrell, the head of the professional theatre company at the University's Krannert Center for the Performing Arts. Burrell was looking for a permanent designer for the company, and Benson was also hired to design and teach in the theatre department. She stayed at the University of Illinois from 1970 to 1974 and eventually designed for the theatre, opera and dance departments all sharing the Krannert Center at the time.

Also in 1966, Benson met Michael Bawtree, who was head of the theatre program at Simon Fraser University in British Columbia. He was one of the first people to give her work in Canada and was extremely important in helping her launch her career. When Benson and her husband, lighting designer Michael J. Whitfield, wanted to return to Canada from Illinois in 1974, she wrote to Bawtree, who was then working at the Stratford Festival. He invited them both to design *The Summoning of Everyman* and *The Medium* at the Third Stage (now the Tom Patterson Theatre), thus beginning Benson's long association with the Stratford Festival. He also asked her to design the costumes for *The Rivals* in New York at the Roundabout Theatre[3] and to teach at the Banff Centre for the Arts. He has continued to support her throughout her career.

Benson is sincerely grateful to these people who first had faith in her work and advises anyone developing a career in the arts to remember the contacts they make in their early years. The theatre is a very small world and supporters and like-minded collaborators should be highly valued as they form the basis of a strong and lasting career. As Brutus observes in Shakespeare's *Julius Caesar*,

> 'Tis a common proof,
> That lowliness is young ambition's ladder,
> Whereto the climber-upward turns his face;
> But when he once attains the upmost round,
> He then unto the ladder turns his back,
> Looks in the clouds, scorning the base degrees
> By which he did ascend. (2.1.22)

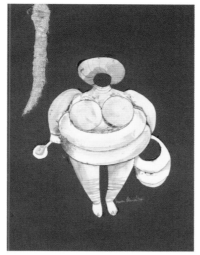

Left: designs for a Courtesan, Luce and Adriana, *The Comedy of Errors*, Krannert Center, University of Illinois, 1974.

Above: two preliminary sketches for the same production.

Opposite: designs for the White Queen, the Carpenter and the Red Queen in *Alice Through the Looking Glass*, Theatre Centre, Windsor, 1969–70.

Design for Blaine Parker as Sebastian in
Twelfth Night, Stratford Festival, 1975.

Opposite: design for K. Lype O'Dell as
Vladimir Lenin in *Travesties*, Manitoba
Theatre Centre, 1979.

CONTRIBUTION TO CANADIAN THEATRE

As stated previously, Benson found it very difficult to break into Canadian theatre. There was little professional theatre or theatre design work in 1966 when she began. Designers were often local artists or craftspeople struggling to make a living. Benson was one of the first artists who chose to make her career as a theatre designer in this country, but the years from 1966 to 1970 (before she went to the Krannert Center in Illinois) were hard. She worked as a freelance designer in Vancouver and then was hired by the Theatre Centre in Windsor, Ontario, where she designed productions such as *The Comedy of Errors*, *Alice Through the Looking Glass*, *The Miser*, *A Midsummer Night's Dream*, among many others, from 1969 to 1970.

The '60s and '70s were a time of great development in theatre and the arts in Canada, and when Benson returned from the United States in 1974, many more theatres had been established across the country. The years 1974 to 1977 saw her designing at the National Arts Centre, Theatre New Brunswick, Neptune Theatre in Halifax and the Roundabout Theatre in New York City. In 1974, she also began her long association with the Stratford Festival.

Like many other immigrants, Susan Benson has made a huge contribution to her chosen country and developed a well-deserved reputation. She was always interested in teaching and mentoring and, in 1980, she was asked by John Hirsch, Artistic Director of the Stratford Festival, to become Head of Design. Through this position, Benson worked to raise the standard of excellence in theatre and design at Stratford. She also insisted on hiring and training Canadian designers. The Stratford Festival is a unique place to work and places different demands on designers, especially those used to working in smaller regional Canadian theatres. Benson's idea was to hire apprentices from around the country who could learn from assisting more experienced designers and also be mentored on their first designs. Here she was given the chance to pass on her own knowledge and experience of the art of designing for the theatre to a new generation of artists. Most of these former assistants have gone on to successful careers of their own and are indebted to Benson for the opportunity she gave them. She played a leading role in the Stratford Festival's growth, giving aspiring Canadian artists and technicians a place to learn and work at a world class level.

Design for Denise Fergusson as
Fraulein Schneider in *Cabaret*.
Stratford Festival, 1987.

2 Not Just a
Pretty Picture

THOUGHTS ON SET AND COSTUME DESIGN

The designer is primarily a visual artist and not a technician. — SUSAN BENSON

The process of theatrical design is often misunderstood, even within the theatre itself. Rather than seeing the designer as the creator of a visual narrative that shapes and enriches the dramaturgy of a production, theatrical designers are often thought of simply as technicians who realize a director's vision. This implies that the job is to provide a solution to a problem where a set, costumes or lighting must be provided to "suit" the play as specified by the script or the director without any recognition of the designer as a creative partner in the shaping of a production. It is important to recognize the designer's role as much more significant than the mere provision of light, sound, decor or clothing for the actors. That is the end result, but the process of getting to this point requires a great deal of creativity and imagination.

The ephemeral nature of a design, the fact that it exists only within the time and space of a performance, may be one of the reasons the job of a designer is unclear. Photos, sketches and models are all that remain once a production is over, and it is easy to see how these can be mistaken for a final product. In fact, it's possible to do beautiful set or costume renderings and be a bad designer. Although models and sketches are essential as communication tools in the realization of a set, costumes or lighting, the real worth of the design is seen only during the performance itself, in the creation of fleeting moments in time and space, where the design is an integral part of the experience of the audience.

Design for Graeme Campbell as Jamie in *A Long Day's Journey Into Night*, Stratford Festival, 1980.

Preliminary sketch for *Jeanne*, Birmingham Repertory Theatre / Kenwright productions, 1985.

COSTUME DESIGN The role of the costume designer is unique and should not be confused with that of a fashion designer. A costume designer creates a character, not a costume or a line of clothing for sale to fashion-conscious consumers. Although costume designers are aware of both current and historical modes and manners of dress, the creation of a costume comes through an understanding of a character and that character's place within the play, both physical and metaphoric. This means that a costume is not imposed upon an actor but is created as a response to an understanding of the character the actor is playing and knowledge of that character's role within the play. Designers must be able to know not only how it feels to play that particular role but also how the character will appear to, and be interpreted by, the audience. They must be able to see the production as a whole, where every character has a place in the overall image but is also created in great detail. This means that as much attention is paid to buttons and small accessories as it is to the overall look and meaning of the costume in a scene.

Costume design serves many functions. Not only does it clarify and enhance the work of the actor in their creation of a character, but it can also speak volumes about the deeper meanings in the play and set a mood and locale. A design is constantly moving in concert with the actors and the narrative of the play. At times costumes need to add life and colour to a scene, while sometimes they need to fade into the background. A "good" or a "bad" costume can be judged only in terms of the actor and the script as presented within the production. A good design can be speculated upon only by looking at a costume rendering. Until it comes to life through the actor in performance, it is only an empty shell. Creating the costume sketch is the starting point for the design. From then on the designer is working in three dimensions with the cutter and actor to create the perfect clothes for that character, which are then enhanced through accessories such as jewellery, hats, wigs and shoes.

26

SET DESIGN The set designer creates the physical and metaphoric space of the play that, like the costume design, is integral to the performance. The "setting" begins with the empty stage space and not only responds to physical needs in the text but also communicates information about the play to an audience visually: historical period, time of day, locale and so on. The physical setting that is created onstage is directly related to the movement of the actors, but the set also works in tandem with lighting, sound and costume to enhance and support the actors and the deeper meanings of the play. Sometimes the set and costumes work together harmoniously in the play, and sometimes they are in direct contrast. These are all conscious choices that must be discussed and carefully developed.

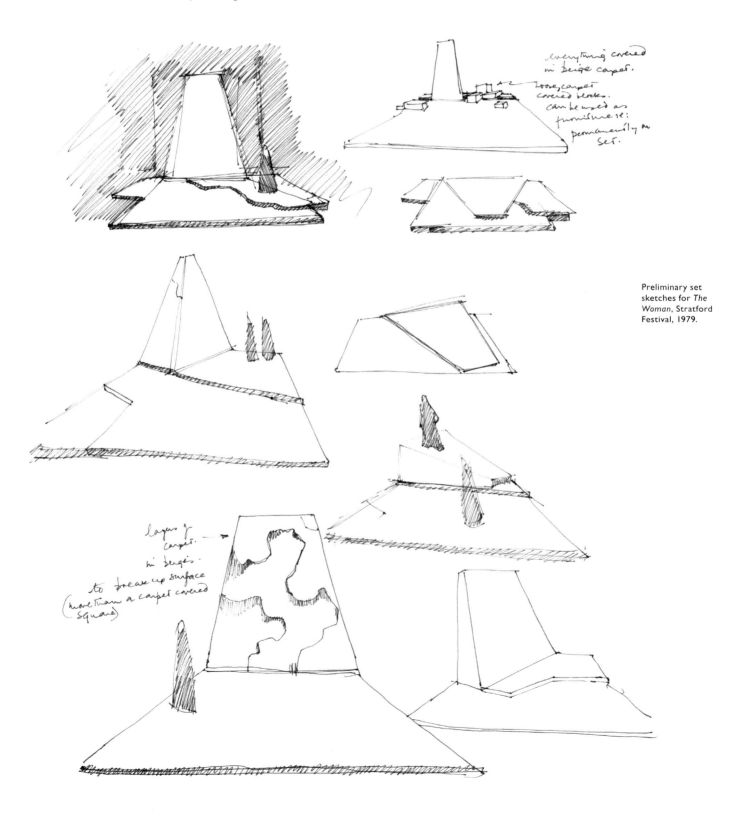

Preliminary set sketches for *The Woman*, Stratford Festival, 1979.

ENTRANCE OF
TAMINO (FOREST)

SERPENT

QUEEN OF NIGHT
ENTRANCE

MOVING SILK PANELS
MOVED FROM GALLERY
LEVEL

SILK PAINTED "CHINESE"
SERPENTS WORKED BY 8 MEN

THROUGH TRAP - VERY TALL
STRONG LIGHTS FROM UNDER
FLOOR

SARASTRO
ARRIVAL

Sc 18 SARASTRO
ARRIVAL

Act 2 SARASTRO +
PRIESTS

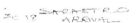
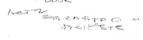

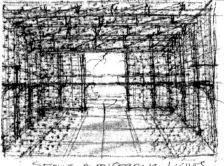  

SMOKE AND STRONG LIGHTS
WINDOWS IGNITE SIDE TO
SIDE

SARASTRO RIDING ON
INLAID BRONZE AND BLACK WAGON
2:16

SILK BANNERS + PAINTED BANNERS
DROP FROM GALLERIES

Sc 15
OLD WOMAN

3 BOYS IN "FLYING MACHINE"

14. LIONS.

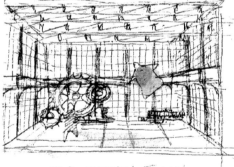 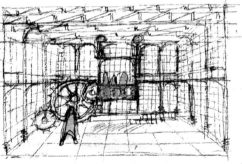 

OLD WOMAN FLOWN
OUT

3 BOYS FLY IN ON
"INDUSTRIAL" WAGON

RED PAINTED SILK CHINESE
LIONS

TRIAL BY FIRE
AND
WATER

2:28

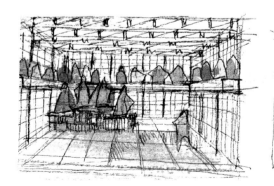 

SMOKE AND
FLAMES THROUGH
CENTER OF
BRONZE DOOR

FIRE = PAINTED SILK
= MOLTEN METAL "TIPPED"
FROM CAULDRON
WATER = PAINTED SILK
TUMBLES FROM CAULDRON
SMOKE

Storyboard for *The Magic Flute*, Minnesota Opera/Dallas Opera, 1997.

1:9
MONOSTATOS
"ROOM"

"TENT" OF CLOTHES

1:15
TEMPLE
ENTRANCE OF 3 BOYS

BRONZE WALL
3 SILVER/BRONZE FRAMES
TRACK ONSTAGE

1:16/7

SHAFTS OF EERIE LIGHTING
FOR MONOSTATOS AND SLAVES

2:2 TEST OF SILENCE

MOVING COGS

2.7

GOBOS/DAPPLE

SC.13
ARIA OF NIGHT
PAMINA MONOSTATOS

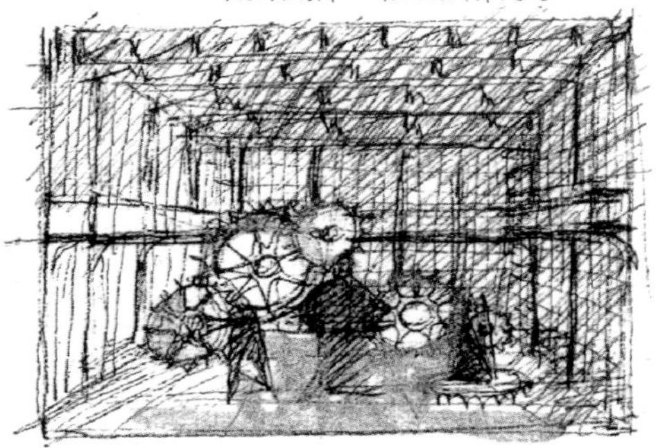

PUFN UP THROUGH
TRAP.

SILK BANNERS DROPPED
FROM GIRDERS

SC.23

GOBLET UP ON
TRAP

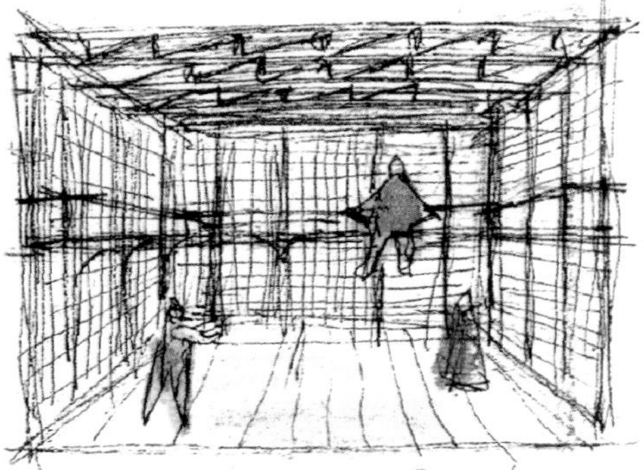

BATTENS FLOWN
OUT?

2:30

WINDOWS START TO SLIDE
OPEN

FINALE.

SET OPENS UP
WITH LIGHT. LARGE
BRONZE COG FLIES

A WAY OF WORKING

I regard the theatre as the greatest of all art forms, the most immediate way in which a human being can share with another the sense of what it is to be a human being. — THORNTON WILDER

Susan Benson's exceptional humanism, her respect for and fascination with humanity, can be seen not only in how she approaches her design work but also in the way she works with others. It is no coincidence that she is also an outstanding portrait artist as well as a theatre designer as her focus is always on the human being behind the story. Even the smallest role in a production is regarded with special care as Benson finds that it is often in the small parts, particularly in larger productions, that a story is told visually.

In theatre, ballet and opera, her understanding of the play always begins with the characters created by the writer and brought to life by the performer. She not only loves to work closely with these performers in creating a role, but also knows the success of her work depends on the collaboration amongst a team of fellow artists and technicians, each with a unique perspective. It is impossible to speak to her about her work without a reference to the inspiring creative contribution of fellow artists and technicians who have helped bring her ideas to life. Research for this book began with a long list of people to contact, all of whom brought something special to a particular production. Some of their stories appear throughout this book.

Benson prefers to work in a situation where everyone on the production is important, respected and encouraged to give their best. She believes that creativity cannot happen without openness and laughter where the imagination is free to try new ideas. To this end, her design sketches, though very precise in terms of character, line and colour, leave room for interpretation by others working to bring the play to life.

ATTENTION TO DETAIL When working with actors in developing a character, Benson finds attention to detail is essential in the onstage world she has created. She feels there is no room for an attitude of "that will do," but strives to work to the best of her ability no matter what the circumstances.

This can be seen particularly in her insistence on small details in costume and props often seen only by the actors. When an actor opens a drawer, there will be dressing inside that fits the needs of the plays and can mean the world to the actor. Undergarments such as corsets and petticoats, never seen by the audience, will have details appropriate to the character as her work supports and enhances the actor's role. She is also tireless in finding the right fabric or costume detail for each show. She sees the design for a play as an overall pattern that has to be right as every detail contributes to the whole. If the details aren't right, the entire shape and progress of the play suffers. She feels fortunate to have learned about the need for detail from excellent cutters, directors and performers she has worked with over the years.

COLOUR AND TEXTURE Benson's attention to details extends to her unique use of colour and texture in design, particularly costuming. Trained as a painter, she sees each play as a moving painting where the colour palette changes with the needs of each scene, in concert with the lighting. She uses colour to express time, mood, character and locale as a nuanced support to the meaning in the text. Colour choices are determined by both research and intuitive response to the play script. In opera or dance it is also determined by the music, as colour is a direct response to the tempo and tone of the music. Colour and shape are particularly important when designing for large theatres where details are lost from a distance.

This use of colour as a living element that complements the action can be seen particularly in her work with director Brian Macdonald in productions such as *The Mikado*, *The Gondoliers* and *Iolanthe*. Macdonald used Benson's colour palettes for each play to shape his choreography. Performers and dancers would often have

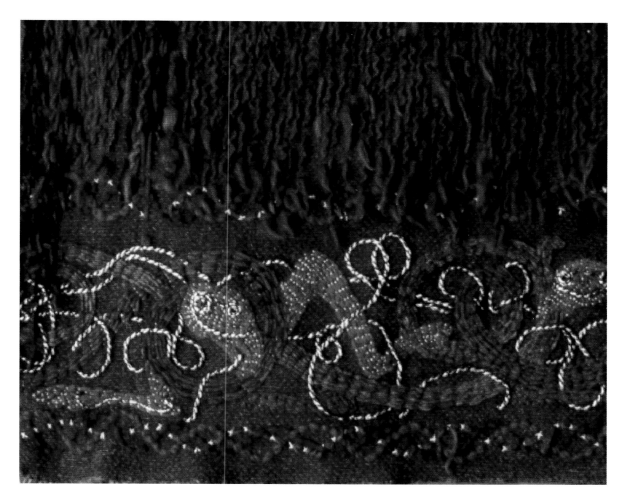

Designs for *Macbeth*, Stratford Festival, 1983, clockwise from top: detail of Duncan's tabard; Nicholas Pennell in the title role; detail of Macbeth's armour decoration, created by Vera Hrdlicka.

fabric or colour samples attached to their rehearsal clothes to enable Macdonald to create visual compositions as he directed the play.

Benson's early training and exposure to superior craftsmanship applied to clothing have led her to develop many different techniques for costume treatment. Special dyeing and texturing of theatre costumes often result from the need to recreate period fabric and trim that no longer exist in the modern world. It is also a way to enhance a fabric so it has richness and depth under stage lighting and, sometimes, to create a sense of age and wear.

In post-war England, theatre designers and craftspeople were faced with enormous shortages. They often had to create the illusion of sumptuous fabric and clothing from very little. This led to a long tradition of fabric manipulation and treatment that Benson first saw at the Royal Shakespeare Theatre in a *The War of the Roses*, designed by John Bury in 1963. Many British designers at the time, such as Bury and Desmond Heeley,[1] had learned these techniques from influential designer Oliver Messel. From these roots, Benson developed her own approach to fabric manipulation, informed by her early training and observation.

Maggie Smith as Hippolyta in *A Midsummer Night's Dream*, Stratford Festival, 1977; detail of Mustardseed's costume in the same production.

A LOST ART? Another perspective on Susan Benson's approach to fabric manipulation is her interest in traditional craft skills such as weaving, beading and embroidery, which are often practised by women. These skills have long been used to add interest and personal touches to clothing. In a theatrical sense, in addition to creating depth, they are a reflection of culture and enhance the story being told about each character. It is interesting that Benson, in the execution of her designs, has preserved and revived these crafts (within the theatrical world), which are sometimes marginalized. Also notable is that most theatre technicians who use these skills in interpreting her designs are women who often have an intuitive understanding of how to lift her designs off the page using such techniques. These specialized artisans are vital to theatrical costuming, and their enormous contributions are often overlooked or underappreciated. In a modern world where time is money, working to this high standard is sometimes impossible. The Stratford Festival, National Ballet and

Canadian Opera Company, where Benson has done so much of this work, are unique, not only in Canada, but also in the Western world for their attention to this kind of detail. Sadly, they are also under great financial pressure and many of these techniques are becoming a lost art.

APPROACHING AND RESEARCHING THE DESIGN Susan Benson begins her work by envisioning the performers onstage — in costume; the setting or world of the play evolves from these visualizations. This focus on the actor, in what is often a deceptively simple setting, results from long hours of research and distillation of ideas. Working at the Stratford Festival, where she saw the effectiveness of Tanya Moiseiwitsch's permanent setting and learned how Moiseiwitsch and Desmond Heeley used the space, influenced her preference for simple settings. Where this may be an obvious choice when designing Shakespeare, the preference for a setting that relies upon the imagination of the audience to complete the world of the play has extended to all of her work. Her marriage to and long-time collaboration with lighting designer Michael J. Whitfield has also influenced her approach. Some people have falsely assumed that Benson is primarily a costume designer because of the emphasis she places on the costumed actor working in the necessary space and light that will best complement the needs of the script. However, her work in set design is consistently outstanding for its seeming simplicity, masking a complex understanding of the spatial and visual needs of the script.

Benson's work on a production begins with many hours of research, both visual and written. She considers this the strength and foundation of her work. Understanding historical background and the layered, complex meaning in the text is just as important as the visual research done for a production. She reads the play many times and creates a series of rough sketches in order to work out ideas and provide a visual basis for discussions with the director. This search is often rewarded by finding just the right reference book or the right object that inspires an approach to the play as the jumping-off point for creation. She will also travel, if necessary, to find the right information or details, as she did in researching her design for *The Crucible* with a trip to Salem, Massachusetts.

She compares design to a beautifully wrapped gift. Many designers can create something that looks lovely on the outside but, once the layers are unwrapped during the performance, it's what's inside that really counts. Beautiful-looking sets and costumes are worthless unless they support and enhance the meaning in the script. To this end, she also feels that theatre artists must be disciplined and first know the play in depth before coming up with any kind of innovative ideas. Too often meaningless images and performances result from a lack of diligence. Only when the play and the writer's intentions are understood, is it possible to create with freedom.

Prop sketch of a doll for *The Crucible*, Stratford Festival, 1975.

Design for Maggie Smith as
Titania in *A Midsummer Night's
Dream*, Stratford Festival, 1977.

"Why" is a very important word in design. The work must have a basis in truth. If designers do not believe in what they are doing, then they cannot ask the audience to believe. Is the work purely decorative. If so, why? Is this what the piece calls for, or is it just the designers being "clever" without any real understanding of the play?

Above all, Benson feels that designers must think and see as artists. They must approach each play as creators and innovators. They must also keep up with contemporary movements in art, film, dance and theatre and constantly explore new ways of expression. She believes that giving oneself the time to dream and experiment is an essential part of creativity; many hours of thought and experimentation must take place before the final design is realized.

COLLABORATION WITH THE DIRECTOR

The single biggest problem in communication is the illusion that it has taken place. — GEORGE BERNARD SHAW

No two designers work in the same way, and every designer will approach a production differently; however, it is impossible to be a solitary artist in the theatre. A designer collaborates with many skilled individuals in the creation of a performance, and one of the key relationships is with the director. Generally, in the initial stages of a production, discussions between the designer and director interpret and shape the world of the play. These critical talks lay the groundwork for how the rest of the production will proceed, but the nature of this collaboration is often misunderstood and rarely written about or discussed. It is also one of the most difficult processes to communicate to others, because it is a very intuitive, non-linear search for understanding and a shared learning experience where all parties grow in trust and work together to bring the play to life. Without collaboration with the director, the creative work of the designer cannot proceed in any effective way. Conversely, without the director's recognition of the integral part the visual and aural elements play in a production, the final presentation will lack depth and dimension.

Susan Benson has worked with directors who have a variety of approaches to and ways of working on a production. She enjoys working with a director who welcomes her contribution; someone she can talk to and feed off. The best directors listen and use what a designer gives them. The hardest relationship is when a director thinks he or she has a good visual sense but doesn't really give the designer enough information to work with. Successful collaboration with a director often means the final result is greater than the sum of its parts. Notable amongst these successful collaborators are Robin Phillips and Brian Macdonald, both visual directors who worked in very different ways.

Robin Phillips, Artistic Director of the Stratford Festival from 1975 to 1980, always had a strong idea of how he wished to approach the production, including its visual aspects. Benson learned much from his work with actors and his understanding of the play. She respected his vision as she felt that choices about the design always arose from a genuine desire to bring the text to life in performance and were never about his ego. Her work with Phillips on *The Woman* (1979) and *A Midsummer Night's Dream* (1976–1977) at the Stratford Festival was particularly memorable for her.

Benson's long working relationship with director and choreographer Brian Macdonald began with a production of *The Mikado* at the Stratford Festival in 1982. This was so successful that they went on to collaborate on several more productions, such as *The Gondoliers* (1983), *Iolanthe* (1984), *Cabaret* (1987), *HMS Pinafore* (1988) and *Guys and Dolls* (1990). Macdonald was a pleasure to work with as he could always see the potential in what she gave him. As a choreographer, he could appreciate Benson's vision of performance as a moving painting.

Susan Benson had designed two productions of *Twelfth Night* when she came to work with Michael Langham[2] on a new production at the Atlantic Theatre Festival. Having done the play before, she felt she was very familiar with the characters, but Langham's analysis of the piece took her to new depths of understanding.

By carefully reading and rereading the lines with Langham, she saw the characters more completely than she had before. Olivia, for example, has a brooch containing her own portrait. What kind of a woman would carry around her own image on a brooch? How would this affect her character and the other decisions she makes about what she wears? By discussing this small detail, she was able to arrive at a far greater understanding of the character.

This same approach, applied to other characters such as the captain of the ship that rescues Viola, helped Benson see them in much more depth. The captain is a minor character with few clues to his character, but he gives Viola the clothes of a gentleman to wear. Where did these clothes come from? And how would he have them in his possession? Perhaps this is not an ordinary sea captain or an ordinary ship? What kind of ship could this be, and how will that influence the clothing worn by the captain and his sailors?

Preliminary rough sketches for all three of Olivia's costumes in *Twelfth Night*, Atlantic Theatre Festival, 1996.

Opposite, clockwise from top left: designs for Ann Baggley as Olivia; Orsino's attendants; Leon Pownall as Feste; Ann Baggley as Olivia.

Early
Greek

Nestor
Head dress.

Preliminary sketches for Stratford Festival production of *The Woman*, 1979. Opposite: *Guys and Dolls*, 1990, and *The Mikado*, 1983.

PULL@CROWDS
COSTUMES.

Monica Wolf, Thomas Barrett, Mary Ann McCormick, Steven Horst, Wendy Nielsen and Craig Ashton in a scene from Cosi Fan Tutti at the Banff Centre, 1991.

3 Putting it All Together

Design for Martha Henry
as Hecuba in *The Woman*,
Stratford Festival, 1979.

Opposite: designs for John
Jarvis as Malcolm; a Witch;
Shaun Austin-Olsen as the
Thane of Ross in *Macbeth*,
Stratford Festival, 1983.

COSTUME RENDERINGS

Susan Benson works with a variety of materials when creating final design sketches and varies her style and choice of materials to best bring a production to life on paper. As she is also a fine artist who paints in oils, she frequently favours this medium for her theatre designs. Putting paint on paper is a mental exercise for her, a way to find the play and its structure. In each rendering, she strives to develop and communicate her understanding of the play. This, she hopes, will then inspire others.

The specific approach Benson chooses for a production evolves from her research and her costume-rendering technique. This, of course, varies for each play as Benson explores the character through paint and colour. Rather than seeing the costume sketch as a simple guideline for construction, she thinks of it as a way of communicating her understanding of the characters in the play. The act of applying paint to paper is a creative means of expression and exploration. Her drawing is then interpreted in consultation with the many talented cutters, jewellers, milliners, painters and dyers she works with. This can be seen particularly in her costume designs for the Stratford productions of Edward Bond's *The Woman* and Shakespeare's *Macbeth*. These are highly evocative costume renderings where fabric and accessories are suggested but open to interpretation. This approach allows others to bring their own vision to the final realization of the costume.

Designs for dancers Laura Graham and John Kaminski, and Evelyn Hart and Barry Watt in *Steps*, Royal Winnipeg Ballet, 1986.
Opposite: designs for David Keeley as Bill Sikes and Susan Gilmour as Nancy in *Oliver*, Citadel Theatre, Edmonton, 1993.

A design is not complete until Benson feels all elements work together as a whole. For her, each play has a rhythm or a pattern where every costume and accessory has a purpose. Once she feels this has been achieved, the real work of bringing the sketch to life begins.

Creating the costume sketch is the starting point for the design. From then on the real work with the cutter and the actor begins. This work is complemented by the many fabric painters, dyers, jewellers, milliners and wigmakers who help in the creation of the ideal costume for that character. To this end, Benson does many detailed wig, jewellery and hat drawings in addition to the main costume sketch.

Whatever role the actor is playing has to be developed individually. Costume creation takes place in a number of fittings. This is where the shape and details of the individual costume are established. Often the process for the designer and the cutter is similar to creating a piece of sculpture. There is a quiet intensity in a costume fitting where a creative rapport among the actor, designer and cutter must be established. Many times, the design has to be adapted from the original character created on paper. The costume must be shaped to make it suitable for the actor playing the part, both for his or her individual shape and proportions and especially for character and period. The fitting must allow time for experimentation and mistakes. First and foremost, the designer tries to make the actors feel at home in their clothes while, at the same time, she is balancing colour, tonal value, texture and detail related to the overall look of the show. Often it is the crowd and secondary characters who tell the story visually — the extras who surround the principals give texture and colour to the play as a whole. Thus, it is very important that these characters are dressed correctly for the play; otherwise, they can pull focus from the principals. Another important aspect of fittings is that every feature of the performer's clothing must be present. Boots, shoes, wigs, jewellery, trim, braid and even props need to be worked into the overall creation of the character.

Concept sketches for an alternative production of *The Mikado* (never produced). Opposite: design for Slaves in *The Magic Flute*, Minnesota Opera/ Dallas Opera, 1997; design for Market People in *Romeo and Juliet*, National Ballet of Canada, 1995. Layouts of this kind are very useful for the designer and director to gain an overview of the production and look at character and colour balance.

A TRIBUTE TO CYNTHIA MACLENNAN BY SUSAN BENSON

I do not believe that she ever had her photograph or bio in any of the programs; her name was in small print at the back. She did not appear on the stage or have much publicity. She didn't have an office with a door, and she didn't have a secretary. She was a "cutter." She had a large cutting table with her shears (which you DID NOT touch). She had a first hand and a team of incredible sewing ladies, and she stood at that table most of the day but ...

She had a touch like gossamer. She knew the body and how to achieve a good fit without the designer having to think about it. She was someone who was revered by designers from across the globe; someone who helped to establish the extremely high standards for a theatre company which was renowned in Europe and North America for the quality of its work. The Stratford Festival was the zenith for designers because of the standards which Cynthia set and the way that the designs were interpreted. Her standards affected countless other cutters and many designers across Canada. Her influence was incalculable. Her costumes were the scenery for the actors. Nothing else was needed for the Festival stage other than the lights, the props and the actors. Images of her costumes will stick in the minds of theatregoers for many years: Maggie Smith in the glorious dresses designed by Robin Fraser Paye for *As You Like It*, and the simple beautiful clothes that Daphne Dare designed for Martha Henry in Robin Phillips' 1975 production of *Measure for Measure*.

Cynthia created costumes for so many actors and actresses who appeared at the Festival: Jessica Tandy, Nicholas Pennell, William Hutt, Brian Bedford, Domini Blythe, Marti Maraden, Barry MacGregor, Jeremy Brett — there are too many to mention.

She always treated fabrics as you would in everyday life — never flattening a light fabric onto something so that you lost the quality of the fabric. The clothes looked as though they had never been touched. She knew all aspects of period cutting and construction so that the designer's work was interpreted perfectly.

I had designed many productions before I came to the Stratford Festival and, when I was interviewed by Artistic Director, Robin Phillips in 1974, I remember being asked why I wanted to work there. I think that I must have given at least one correct reply when I said that I wanted to see what happened to my designs when they were built by brilliant people, and Cynthia MacLennan was brilliant. I think I can say that Robin revered the production people, and I can remember many times coming into the wardrobe in the evening and finding him sitting with Cynthia at her table — sewing! I don't think that there are many artistic directors who could, or would, do that.

Designers like Tanya Moiseiwitsch, Desmond Heeley, Daphne Dare and Ann Curtis were her special friends and colleagues, perhaps because their knowledge was equal to hers. She taught many of us who were new to the Festival so much about costumes, and few people could teach her anything she didn't already know. She had an extraordinary knowledge of the history of clothing and construction. She taught me so many things: choice of fabric — you did not dare present her with a piece of fabric that would not work for a particular costume; it would be pushed to one side, and you would feel rather embarrassed at even thinking you could get it by her.

One of the first things that opened my eyes to the importance of detail was Cynthia asking me to find a fabric suitable to cover one of the corsets for a show that I had designed. The corset would never be seen by the audience, but Cynthia said that the first thing that an actor did when getting ready for a performance was to put on their underpinnings. An actress playing a whore would not be helped into character if the first thing she put on was a corset and chemise covered in plain white cotton. A luridly coloured brocade-covered corset decorated with tatty lace could help to create the world the actress was entering in her characterization. A man's shirt with deep rich lace on the cuffs said that this person was wealthy and thought about his clothes, but in a totally different way from someone with no lace at all on his shirt. All of these details, all of this care and attention, added to what happened on the stage — the unseen things which are very difficult to quantify but brought a depth and quality to what the audience saw onstage and added to the reputation of the theatre being the best classical company in North America. Some people may think that this was an extravagant approach and an unnecessary waste of money, but I think that if you were to ask the actors who worked with her they would certainly not agree with that assessment.

I do not think there was ever a case where her costumes had to be rebuilt, did not fit, or were unsuitable. Her careful, thoughtful approach meant that there were very few notes that needed to be taken once her costumes were onstage. She said that the skill of fitting costumes perfectly to actors' bodies came from her time working as a cutter for the ballet, where clothes have to fit well in order to allow the dancer to move. If a costume needed to look heavy, she could achieve this but would insist that the fabrics were never so heavy as to impede the actor. She was one of the few cutters in whom I had complete confidence. If I was unable to be present during the building period, my costumes would appear onstage exactly as I would have wanted them. Her choices, her eye, her sense of the style of the piece were perfection.

She was meticulous and her fittings were sacrosanct. The designer and assistants were invited into the fitting after about twenty minutes of her adjusting the fit of the costume with her first hand and the actor. Quite honestly, I often walked into a first fitting with Cynthia and felt that there was nothing left for me to say because the costume on the actor was perfect. She created sculptures in which the actor could move, be comfortable and feel in character. Designers could create beautiful drawings but we would have been nowhere without Cynthia.

Jessica Tandy as Hippolyta in *A Midsummer Night's Dream*, Stratford Festival, 1976; Nicholas Pennell as Ford in *The Merry Wives of Windsor*, Stratford Festival, 1982. Cynthia MacLennan built both of these costumes from Benson's designs. Pennell's costume, in particular, was a marvel of cutting as it was created with only a single centre-back seam in the body of the doublet.

CYNTHIA MACLENNAN (1933-2009) graduated from the Macdonald Institute in Guelph and launched her career as one of the first costume cutters with the National Ballet of Canada, dressing Founding Artistic Director Celia Franca. During her nearly twenty-year tenure at the Ballet, she also began working for the Stratford Festival, where she spent over forty seasons until her retirement in 1998.

THE STRATFORD FESTIVAL PROPS DEPARTMENT

In her years at the Stratford Festival, Susan Benson enjoyed a close working relationship with Roy Brown and Frank Holte, who shared the head of props position at the Avon and Festival Theatres, respectively. They were both important creative partners in the realization of productions at the Festival. They worked with an amazing group of propmakers with a wide variety of talents. In addition to organizing the shops and controlling the budget, they were both artists in their own right. Benson placed a great deal of trust in their expertise. Both men established a work ethic in the prop shop that put the production first and encouraged designers to have a vision and imagination that would inspire their own creativity.

The prop shop was a combination of technical excellence, hard work and humour that did not suffer fools lightly and where the focus was always on doing the best work possible. If that meant staying late on a project or juggling the budget to build a special prop that a particular show needed, so be it. Working in a large theatre company such as the Stratford can be extremely difficult as the pressure for excellence in all areas must be balanced with time, budget and staff. The Festival prop shop somehow managed to be efficient, mad, eccentric and creative all at the same time. Holte and Brown appreciated Benson's sense of humour and (although they weren't above their own practical jokes) always respected her talent and ability to communicate and filter information from the director and rehearsal. They also appreciated Benson's design sketches as they showed how a prop would be used in context. Unlike a photo from the internet, the sketches illustrated how a prop would be used onstage as part of the overall look of a production – invaluable information that includes the artisans in the shop as partners in the realization of a design. Benson had such respect for their talent that she relied on Brown and Holte to create additional scenic elements when necessary. Roy Brown created the multilayered gold leaf-lacquered floor for *The Mikado* (1982) and Frank Holte, in addition to other projects, is remembered for his creation of "pig poop" — a material used on the doors of the *Julius Caesar* set (1978).

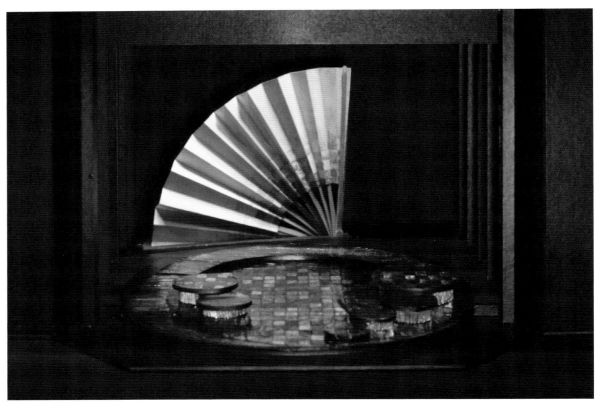

Set model for *The Mikado*, Stratford Festival, 1982.

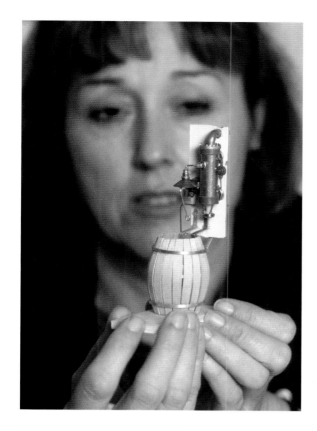

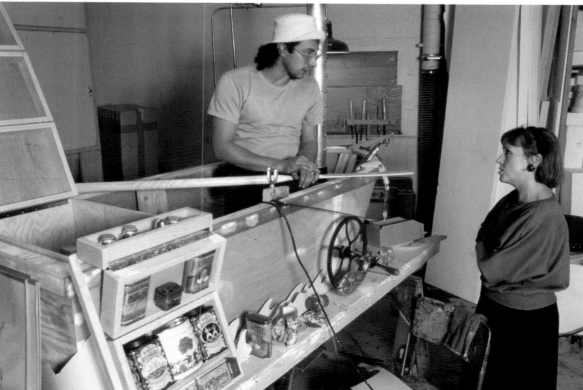

Susan Benson's designs for *HMS Pinafore* at Mirvish Productions in Toronto in 1988 were executed in the Stratford Festival prop shop. Clockwise from top left: Benson with the model piece for a shower unit in the opening scene; with Head of Props Frank Holte; with John LeBerg, building the boat for Little Buttercup's arrival.

Set rendering for *Julius Caesar*, Stratford Festival, 1978.

Design for Maureen
Forrester as Madame
Flora in *The Medium*,
Stratford Festival, 1974.

WORKING WITH PERFORMERS

Nicholas Pennell, with whom Benson worked on several productions at Stratford, understood and greatly respected the designer's role and its importance to his performance. Pennell was one of several intelligent and talented actors she had the pleasure of working with whose focus was always on developing the details of their role along with the designer. Benson knew that when an actor such as Pennell asked for something or had a problem with a prop or costume, it was always about the character and never the ego. Commenting on her work at the Stratford Festival she says,

> If you have actors like Maggie Smith, Stephen Ouimette or William Hutt, they can bring images alive for the audience without the use of elaborate sets, costumes or props. I think that this is what Tyrone Guthrie had in mind when he and Tanya Moiseiwitsch worked on the design for the Festival Stage. "Less is more" has always been a phrase that I have heard in this theatre since I started designing here in 1974. The emphasis was always on the actor. (Benson interview)

From her experience in ballet, Benson learned that dancers as a rule will do everything they can to make a costume work, and, if dancers tell you they can't work in their costumes, you must listen. She also learned from opera singers such as Maureen Forrester, who would never complain and was always open to trying new things. In a production of Gian Carlo Menotti's *The Medium*, at the Stratford Festival's Third Stage,[1] Benson asked Forrester to wear a wig that would make her hair appear thin and badly dyed as well as several layers of heavy lisle stockings that made her beautiful legs look larger and misshapen. As they were right for the character, Forrester embraced the design and brought it to life onstage in spite of the fact that she was performing in the grueling summer heat of a theatre without air conditioning.

Benson with actor Marianne Woods and cutter Sophie Martin in a costume fitting for *HMS Pinafore*, Mirvish Productions, 1988.

Designs for *Blessings in Disguise*, Manitoba Theatre Centre, 1998. Clockwise from top left: Rod Beattie as Father Gustave, Kim Rannie as Sophie, Graham Ashmore as Albert and Martha Henry as Mme Vermillion. Opposite: Martha Henry as Mme. Vermillion.

Sharry Flett as Katharina in *The Taming of the Shrew*, Stratford Festival, 1981.

LOUISE GUINAND, LIGHTING DESIGNER, ON WORKING WITH MICHAEL J. WHITFIELD, BENSON'S PARTNER AND FREQUENT COLLABORATOR

I am honoured and feel privileged to be one of the many, many lighting designers Michael Whitfield has mentored and influenced over the years. As head of lighting design at both the Stratford Festival and the Canadian Opera Company, his influence on an entire generation of Canadian lighting designers has been immeasurable.

We first met when Michael called and interviewed me for a job at the Stratford Festival. I hadn't really applied to work there but, a few days after that half an hour chat, I was offered work as his assistant. I continue to design at the Festival to this day. I feel very fortunate and grateful for the time he took to seek me out and teach me so many things. I spent much of my first year at the Festival looking at his work and observing the finesse that made it so smooth and unique. Michael was very precise in his work but he didn't dictate to his assistants. He gave guidance but we had the freedom to work things out for ourselves.

Often lighting designers feel they must use a lot of coloured gel to create dimension and interest, but Michael was the master of open-white lighting, and I learned how versatile it can be. I still approach design from this base today. Michael used open-white lighting extremely adeptly, and it allowed for the subtle colouring of costumes to be seen. It was fascinating watching Michael and Susan Benson work together, as they did on many shows, with such mutual respect. He is a true painter with light (or maybe "sculptor" is a better word), yet will never change or overwork a look. He is meticulous in his observation of detail yet does not get caught up in it; he always knows where to put the focus and allocate time and energy. He isn't a "showy" kind of designer, but the subtlety of his craftsmanship shines through. I remember how multilayered his work was in *The Tempest*; it was a stunning piece of work. He managed to create such an ambience that you felt the air was full of light. I was amazed at the work he did on that show and how he enhanced Desmond Heeley's design. As a designer, he is always very conscious of the direction of the light, not just the level of illumination. I've never seen a show of his where

I felt there was a superfluous cue; his lighting has a clarity that is never busy, and you're never distracted by it.

Then there's his (in)famous sense of humour. Michael is the master of the pun, and his wordplay has lightened many a tense technical rehearsal. I think it demonstrates how agile his mind is. He is a great communicator who has melded the ability to design with the skill of communicating without imposing his ideas. His focus is always on the needs of the show, not on his own ego.

The cast of *The Woman*, Stratford Festival, 1979.

Michael has been very helpful and supportive to me and many other assistants, giving us the chance to design for ourselves. He recommended me to Robin Phillips when he was artistic director of The Grand Theatre in London. Later, I was hired to co-design the production of John Murrell's *New World* in 1984 with Michael. He taught me a great deal and helped me to launch my own career. He's done the same for many others and the Canadian design community owes a great deal to his leadership, support and talent. I'm very grateful that I was able to work with him and enjoy his support.

Saloon girls

Saloon women

4 Selected Productions

Preliminary designs for *The Ballad of Baby Doe*, San Francisco Opera, 2000.

THE SUMMONING OF EVERYMAN

In 1974 Michael Bawtree asked Benson to return to Canada from Illinois, where she was working at the Krannert Centre for the Performing Arts, to design her first show at the Stratford Festival. Bawtree, whom she first met in 1966, was a champion of her work and asked her to design *The Summoning of Everyman* as an opera by Charles Wilson (based on the medieval mystery play) at the Stratford Festival Third Stage. This was the beginning of her long association with the Stratford Festival which became a home to her and husband Michael J. Whitfield for many years.[1]

This production stands out for Benson as her introduction to the exceptionally talented craftspeople in the Stratford workshops. There was very little money for this production, so they were forced to realize her design with few resources. Used to designing in smaller theatres where she was responsible for providing solutions for every detail of construction, Benson felt supported as never before to act as a creative artist leading a team of craftspeople with her vision. As such, her work on this production was a valuable learning experience. Benson designed simple, basic garments enhanced by dyeing, weaving and macramé. Jewellery and masks were created from found objects: leather scraps, shells, seeds and other things that were easy to obtain. Thanks to the inventiveness of the people working on the show, the final result was beautiful and rich; Benson's costumes brought life and colour to Eoin Sprott's permanent setting of simple rough-hewn wood.

Designs for Eleanor Calbes as Cousin and Phil Stark as Devil. Opposite: design for Alvin Reimer as Goods.

THE SUMMONING OF EVERYMAN

Stratford Festival, Third Stage, 1974
Director: Michael Bawtree
Set and Costume Designer: Susan Benson
Permanent Stage Designer: Eoin Sprott
Lighting Designer: Michael J. Whitfield

Phyllis Mailing as
Paramour and
Garnet Brooks
as Everyman.

Mask for the
character Goods,
created by Nina
Nodwell.

Opposite: Phyllis
Mailing as Paramour
and Garnet Brooks
as Everyman with
members of the
company.

A MIDSUMMER NIGHT'S DREAM

Robin Phillips began initial design discussions for this production by presenting a piece of richly carved golden wood as an example of his feeling for the show, particularly the court scenes. This physical object spoke volumes to Benson about the textural feel of the world of *A Midsummer Night's Dream* and became a jumping-off point for her design. Phillips discussed how he felt this play was a thinly disguised reflection of the Elizabethan court with the Hippolyta/Titania character as Elizabeth I. He also saw the two worlds of the court and the fairies as reflections of each other in a photographic sense, where one was the "negative" of the other; historically, the Elizabethan court had been influenced by the Spanish style of dark clothing offset with rich jewels and embroidery. This tradition led Benson to create a rich, dark, earthbound court of black and gold, based on the Elizabethan tradition of elaborate court masques, contrasted with the light, ethereal world of the fairies. She used her extensive knowledge of the period to reinterpret Elizabethan court life in a more sensual context for the stage. For example: adjustments such as the length of a man's leg in period trunk hose appeared more elegant to the modern eye, as the breeches were cut higher on the sides than was acceptable for an accurate period cut.[2]

As one was an echo of the other, the fairies were also in Elizabethan dress; but, rather than the heavily structured brocades and velvets of the court, their clothing was lighter in construction, colour and choice of fabric. Instead of appearing as fantastical creatures, they were real characters, but in a different context. In this way, the costumes created the difference in the two worlds of the play. Against a simple setting of richly carved wood on the Festival stage, the court in black and gold appeared monumental and stately while the world of the fairies was lighter, less restrained and more sexualized.

Dream offered a unique opportunity as the play was produced twice with two outstanding actors in the lead role: Jessica Tandy in 1976, and Maggie Smith in 1977. Both took very different approaches to the role of

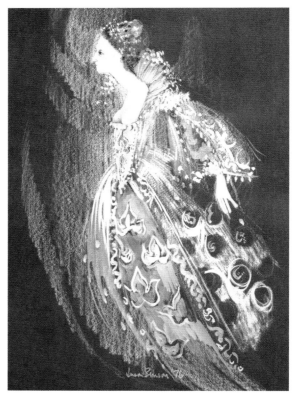

Designs for Jeremy Brett as Oberon and Mia Anderson as Hermia, 1976. Opposite: Alan Scarfe as Bottom and Maggie Smith as Titania, with Bob Baker as Cobweb, Robin Nunn as Peaseblossom and Robert Ruttan as Mustardseed, 1977. Ass's head built by Joy Allan, Stratford Festival prop shop.

A MIDSUMMER NIGHT'S DREAM

Stratford Festival, 1976–77

Director: Robin Phillips

Set and Costume Designer:
Susan Benson

Lighting Designer:
Michael J. Whitfield (1976),
Gil Wechsler (1977)

Clockwise from left: William Needles as
Egeus, Daniel Buccos as a courtier, Robin
Nunn as a courtier, David Fox-Brenton
as a courtier, Jeremy Brett as Theseus,
Jessica Tandy as Hippolyta, Bob Baker as
a courtier, Mia Anderson as Hermia, Tom
Kneebone as Puck and Denise Fergusson
as Helena, 1976.

Hippolyta/Titania, influencing the overall design approach. Benson enjoyed the challenge of rethinking the costume designs to suit the different interpretations of these two actors.

The first production, with Jessica Tandy, was conceived as a masque celebrating the wedding of Hippolyta and Theseus, who resembled Elizabeth I and her lover, the Earl of Essex. Elizabeth fantasizes herself and her lover as Titania and Oberon. An earthbound Hippolyta becomes an ethereal Titania in this vision of herself with Theseus, played by Jeremy Brett. Benson created Tandy's Titania costume to be an almost identical but ethereal version of her court costume but lighter in colour, fabric and treatment. The solid, opaque helmet she wore for the court masque with a black and gold dragon became a more fragile, dreamlike version for Titania, constructed with crin,[3] lace and found objects.

Maggie Smith, in the 1977 production, interpreted Hippolyta as an elegant, older Elizabeth I dreaming about her freer, more sexual youth. Benson used portraits of the young Queen Elizabeth as inspiration for her design for Smith. The costume was interpreted using light, delicate fabrics which were enhanced with beading. Benson used her early experiences with couturier-level beading to embroider the costume herself. The beading gave a more fragile look to the costume as it moved in the light. The more sensual approach to the production this second season required the costumes in the Titania/Oberon scenes to lose the echoes of the Elizabethan masque and the masque headdresses were eliminated.

One of the challenges of a court dressed all in black was how to make it interesting visually. Gayle Tribick, the costume decorator, was instrumental in creating the template for the rich jewellery and embroidery for the court costumes that gave each character individuality and dimension. This template then inspired other wardrobe members to translate the positive Elizabethan court look and structure into the negative dreamworld of the fairies. This vision took much experimentation and development and Benson is grateful for the talent of these people.

Clockwise from top left: designs for Jessica Tandy as Hippolyta, Stephen Russell as a Court Gentleman, Frances Fagan as a Court Lady, David Fox-Brenton as a Court Gentleman and Cathy Wallace as a Court Lady, 1976.

Richard Partington as Demetrius, Denise Fergusson as Helena, Nick Mancuso as Lysander and Mia Anderson as Hermia are discovered in the forest by the court, 1976.

Clockwise from top: detail of Hippolyta's dragon helmet, made by Vera Hrdlicka and worn by Jessica Tandy in 1976; design sketch for the same helmet; design sketch for a candleabra.

Opposite: the lion mask, made by the Stratford Festival prop shop and worn by Bernard Hopkins as Snug the Joiner in 1976 and 1977.

JULIUS CAESAR

In this production, the crumbling empire of Julius Caesar was expressed in simple, striking geometric togas and robes that had a strong sculptural silhouette yet appeared to be breaking apart at the edges as if they were eroding. The basis of each costume was thick, smooth wool cut into simple geometric shapes with decoration simulating various types of crumbling stone.

Gayle Tribick, costume decorator and jeweller, studied geological formations of rock crumbling and splitting. This effect was then recreated in fabric "stone" that was appliquéd to each costume. As the palette for the costumes was a subtle, constrained monochromatic colour scheme, the overall effect was strongly architectural and monumental. This approach was so unique that the costume for Nicholas Pennell as Brutus was chosen as part of the Canadian exhibition at the International Design Quadrennial in Prague. It is significant to note that Benson's designs were chosen a total of five times to represent Canada at the Quadrennial.

Birds of prey were a central theme in the setting on the Stratford Festival stage. Influenced by Cassius' lines in Act V, scene 1, Benson designed large eagles for the upstage areas of the Festival stage. The balcony was removed and replaced by doors in the upstage opening. These were more than eighteen feet high and designed to appear as high relief with images of birds of prey. Frank Holte, head of props for the Festival stage, made these doors by applying a textured material, which he described as "pig poop," carving and treating it to look like metal. The final product was majestic and grand, very far from anything found in a barnyard, no doubt a tribute to Holte's many talents.

Julius Caesar, Act V, Scene 1:

Coming from Sardis, on our former ensign
Two mighty eagles fell, and there they perch'd,
Gorging and feeding from our soldiers' hands;
Who to Philippi here consorted us:
This morning are they fled away and gone;
And in their steads do ravens, crows, and kites
Fly o'er our heads and downward look on us
As we were sickly prey: Their shadows seem
A canopy most fatal, under which
Our army lies, ready to give up the ghost.

JULIUS CAESAR

Stratford Festival, 1978
Director: John Wood
Set and Costume Designer: Susan Benson
Lighting Designer: Michael J. Whitfield

Clockwise from top: Eric Donkin as Julius Caesar, Lorne Kennedy as Metellus Cimber and Nicholas Pennell as Marcus Brutus with members of the company; design for Barbara Stephen as Portia; design for Eric Donkin as Caesar's Ghost. Opposite: design for large upstage centre doors.

THE WOMAN

The Woman, with Martha Henry in the lead role, is set at the end of the Trojan War and influenced by Euripides' play, *The Trojan Women*. Edward Bond's anti-war play features Hecuba, Queen of a decaying Troy, and her struggle to survive against the ravages of war with the Athenians. She is eventually cast out in disgrace along with Ismene, sister of the Athenian general Heros.

Benson focused her design on the changing appearance of the two opposing sides in the war. At the beginning of the play, she used a vibrant palette, rich textures and exotic jewellery to portray the decaying Trojan empire. This was contrasted with the earthy leather, antique pleating and painted armour of their Athenian opponents. As the play progresses, the look of the two sides is reversed. Hecuba and Ismene, originally enemies, join together on a desert island and their clothing becomes earthier, worn out and closer to the people. In contrast, the Athenian soldiers appear in hard-edged, ceremonial armour, underlining their status as victors in the war.

Benson envisioned the world of the play as a wasteland of destruction and plague. This was an interesting case where a rendering technique influenced her approach to the entire design. She experimented with creating a feeling of texture by "dribbling" thin oil paint onto gessoed boards and then wiping and sponging into the oils. This resulted in an evocative costume sketch with little detail but a rich sense of the feeling for the

texture in the clothing. She was fortunate to have a talented support team in the Stratford costume shop who understood what she intended. They brought her renderings to life using various weaving, dyeing and fabric manipulation techniques on a combination of raw silk, linen and open-weave fabrics. The outcome was extremely gratifying as Benson felt the support she had on this production enabled her to realize her initial vision of the production and improve techniques in texturing and dyeing that she experimented with in earlier shows such as *The Summoning of Everyman*.

Lisa Hughes in particular, who was in charge of costume painting and treatment, made a significant contribution to bringing the costume sketches to life, particularly in the second part of the play, where Hecuba and Ismene are marooned on an island and their clothing must appear to be aged, distressed and bleached away with seawater.

To further enhance the idea of rank and status in the play, Gayle Tribick created jewellery in large geometric shapes, based on research from Heinrich Schliemann's discovery of Troy in the late 19th century.

William Hutt as Nestor. Opposite: design for Bill Copeland as the Chief Architect.

THE WOMAN

Stratford Festival, Avon Theatre, 1979
Directors: Peter Moss and Urjo Kareda
Set and Costume Designer: Susan Benson
Lighting Designer: Michael J. Whitfield

GILBERT AND SULLIVAN

In 1982, John Hirsch, artistic director of the Stratford Festival, felt it would enhance the season by adding a production of one of Gilbert and Sullivan's operettas. As their work was no longer bound by copyright, it meant the Festival could reimagine these works in a new way. He chose *The Mikado* and hired Susan Benson to work with choreographer and director Brian Macdonald. It was the beginning of a long and happy partnership that spanned many years.

THE MIKADO

Originally written in 1896, the operetta was never intended as an accurate depiction of life in Japan but rather a satirical look at British society thinly disguised as another culture. The original script, a Victorian interpretation of old Japan seen through European eyes, posed several design challenges; principally, how to create a respectful reflection of Japanese culture seen through a satirical Western perspective and, on a more practical level, how does one dance in a kimono and platform sandals?

Benson approached the show with her usual thorough research. In the pre-internet world of the 1980s, she found it especially difficult to find much useful research material and was delighted to happen upon two large books on Japan in the back of a Korean grocery store on Spadina Avenue in Toronto. These became essential to her interpretation of the production. She was particularly drawn to illustrations of Japanese screens in the books. Expanding her research, she also explored Victorian children's book illustrations: their flat, decorative quality was reminiscent of Japanese woodcuts, and the colour palette was bright without being overdone or crude. Her final design blended these elements with the Art Nouveau style of the early 20th century.

The Set

Benson and Macdonald were keen to breathe new life into the piece and move away from more traditional interpretations. Macdonald wanted the production to be beautiful and flexible. In line with Benson's idea of a performance as a moving painting, they worked together to create a design that moved and flowed as the story developed. Benson, in her role of head of design, wished to encourage young designers and asked Douglas McLean, then an assistant at the Festival, to be co-designer of the set. McLean was instrumental in working out many of the technical details of the final show which appeared simple and elegant but had a great deal of complex design and technical work behind it.

At the time, the Avon theatre stage at the Stratford Festival had a permanent black surround created by Artistic Director Robin Phillips. All productions at the Avon that year were designed to work within this "black box." The structure demanded simple, bold designs that would have visual impact while sustaining focus on the actors. Benson found this an interesting challenge rather than a restriction as it forced her to become even more inventive. She began by doing a series of sketches exploring simple and imaginative ways to change the scenery. After several attempts, she arrived at the idea of small round platforms, reminiscent of Japanese lacquered boxes, which could move and create different configurations. These seven oval "lily pads" of various sizes and heights floated on a larger golden disc and worked together to form a stairway or exist separately. This allowed the show to be very adaptable and fluid in motion in response to Macdonald's directorial and choreographic needs. These movable units were particularly challenging to build as the stage floor of the Avon is raked, or sloped, from the back of the stage to the front.

THE MIKADO

Stratford Festival, 1982
Director and Choreographer: Brian Macdonald
Musical Director: Berthold Carrière
Set Designers: Susan Benson and Douglas McLean
Costume Designer: Susan Benson
Lighting Designer: Michael J. Whitfield

Chorus of School-girls, 1982.

Henry Ingram as Nanki-Poo,
with the ensemble, 1982.

Clockwise from top left: designs for Eric
Donkin as Ko-Ko, Gidon Saks as the
Mikado of Japan, Allen Stewart-Coates as
Pish-Tush, and Christina James as Katisha.

82

Clockwise from top left: Christina James as Katisha; Richard McMillan as Pooh-Bah; Marie Baron as Yum-Yum; Eric Donkin as Ko-Ko, 1982.

Benson based the scenic painting on Japanese screens that looked like polished tortoiseshell squares: all alike yet different, forming a subtle checkerboard pattern. On the set model she used aluminum foil lacquered over with sepia and orange inks, which added golden tones to the floor and movable units — all edged with a glossy black paint. To create the stage, Roy Brown, head of the Avon prop shop, combined paint, gold leaf and lacquer in layers, working with texture and direction to create a jewel-like floor with depth and dimension.

This simple, yet visually stunning basic setting allowed for additional scenic elements, drawn from iconic Japanese images, such as a large fan, a twisted bamboo tree, a moon and the Mikado's palanquin to have a strong visual impact on the changing scenes in concert with the costumes and lighting.

> Susan and I worked on the various "tile" patterns for the floor and pod tops. We made "blocks" using corrugated cardboard mounted on plywood and stamped the patterns using various gold paints. This along with mylar strips formed the basis for the set pieces. The whole surface was then sprayed with a non-glare varnish-fixative in several coats. As far as the props, it was trial and error but always rewarding something; very rare these days. (Roy Brown Interview)

Props

McLean's and Benson's simple, striking set demanded a similar approach to the props for the show. Roy Brown supervised the creation of a number of seemingly simple yet complex props to complement the changing action. Props as straightforward as the fans used by the chorus of "Gentlemen of Japan" were extremely labour-intensive. They needed to appear to be beautiful paper fans yet sturdy enough for vigorous use; able to snap open and closed on cue. Ordinary purchased fans wouldn't stand up to this kind of use, so many hours of research and experimentation with a blow torch, invisible tape and paint ensued — no simple task. The women's fans and parasols were designed and painted to go with their costumes and required the same level of sturdiness as the men's fans while appearing light and delicate. Many versions of these props were experimented with before the final prototype was created.

A twisted bamboo tree became a central prop in the show, posing several practical problems. It had to be carried; it had to be strong; it had to be put together and taken apart on stage with ease; and the actor Eric Donkin, in his role as Ko-Ko, had to sit in it and sing "Tit willow, Tit willow." Benson's design was made up of many curved lines for the trunk and branches, and miles of cane of different sizes had to be bent onto a metal frame. The branches were then adorned with a large number of silk cherry blossoms. In contrast to the tree, they required a delicate touch and artist's eye in order to look natural. Benson is extremely grateful to Stewart Robertson, Georges Kamm and Frank Holte for their work and the talented members of the Stratford Festival prop shop whose contribution to this show was outstanding and a true tribute to their talent. (Benson Interview)

Costumes

Benson's costumes for *The Mikado* emphasized the complex interplay of love and power in the play by contrasting the beauty and delicacy of the female characters with the power and strength of the men. All of the men had wide, horizontal shoulder pieces, based on the traditional Katiginu, which increased their visual strength and power. They also wore "Hakama" — traditional Japanese trousers — made from silk tussah and duppioni. Rehearsal versions of both trousers and wings were a necessity because it took some time to practise kneeling and then jumping up wearing the Hakama and manoeuvring with the added width of the wings. For the women, rather than opting for historically accurate fitted kimonos, Benson designed beautiful flowing robes with trains influenced by the Art Nouveau style of the time.[4] The traditional obi added to these robes became more like a Victorian corset, reinforcing the idea of a Western perspective on Japanese dress.

The kimonos for the principal characters were one of the most striking elements of the production. As each kimono was created with many yards of fabric, these large expanses of cloth became a canvas upon which Benson could design patterns — inspired by Japanese artists such as Kitagawa Utamaro — to suit each character.

While the men's kimonos had strong, rich colours and patterns, the women's chorus and "three little maids from school" were in pastels. The entire production palette was carefully chosen to contrast and change in a variety of character combinations in scenes. To facilitate this physically, special rehearsal costumes with trains were built to approximate the final kimonos, giving the performers and director the time to incorporate the costumes into the choreography. In addition, pieces of coloured fabric were attached to each garment so the director, Brian Macdonald, could compose visually as he choreographed. Another advantage for this production was that the rehearsal hall and fitting rooms were close together. This allowed for a constant rapport among director, designer and performer as rehearsals and fittings progressed.

One of the most challenging aspects of costuming for the show was the creation of the shoes. Dancing on a raked stage with long, flowing silk costumes in footwear that appeared as traditional Japanese socks (tabi) and sandals with a thong was not practical; achieving this illusion took a lot of trial and error. First, the sole of each sandal had to be soft so the shoes would be relatively quiet as the performers danced. Then the thong between the toes had to be both durable and comfortable as the actors moved quickly on a sloped surface. The biggest challenge was keeping the shoes on the performers' feet. A series of white tapes were devised, criss-crossing from where the thongs ended, around the ankles, and a special fastening was created. It took ages for these to be developed, and it took even longer for the Mikado's, Katisha's and Pooh-Bah's shoes to be created as the soles were built up like ancient Greek kothornoi.[5] The outside of the soles then had to be covered with fabric matching each costume. This was a true challenge for members of the shoe department, who deserve high praise for their fortitude and inventiveness.

Makeup

Makeup for the male chorus and many of the female characters was approached as if the performers were putting on a mask rather than attempting any kind of accurate "Japanese" look. The strong horizontal line of the men's shoulder pieces was repeated in strong horizontal eyebrows, but overall the makeup was a slightly exaggerated version of a European face. Actors used a pale base and small lips, but otherwise the approach was as traditional Western stage makeup. Benson varied her rendering technique for the makeup sketches, using pastels in place of watercolour, as she wanted a medium that was closer to actual makeup. Pastel colours blended more easily, and the overall effect was softer.

Brian Macdonald
on *The Mikado*

I remember in *The Mikado*, Susan
wrote the colour of each costume
on a piece of paper with a swatch
of material and attached it to the
rehearsal skirts so I could compose
the stage pictures as I was directing.
She works on this level of detail.
We also tricked everybody in that
show. Japanese women's kimonos are very tight by tradition and
the wearer must hold their knees
together but I asked Susan for something very flowing. My mother,
who was Irish, had been in London
and she said, "Oh, those English
girls were so beautiful in the Gilbert
and Sullivan." Even in her 80s she
remembered this so I asked Susan
for elegance, flow and beauty.

Fittings are very important to Susan;
that's where she does her painterly
bits. We had a big rehearsal room
that was about twenty-five feet
away from the fitting rooms. After
a fitting, Susan would send a mes-
sage to me saying, "Come look at
this." I would stop rehearsal and
show everyone what so and so was
going to look like. The performers
loved it — it gave them a boost.
All the women knew before opening that they looked lovely and the
men looked so handsome. I loved
watching all of that.

John Avey as The Mikado of Japan, in a
tenth-anniversary revival production,
Stratford Festival, 1993. Opposite: Richard
March, a chorus member in the original
1982 production, with wig mistress, Doreen
Freeman, demonstrating the makeup and
wig transformation required to become a
Gentleman of Japan.

Overall Design

One of the special aspects of working on this show for Benson was the time allowed for research and development of ideas. This production in particular was technically demanding, and a great deal of credit is due to the Stratford Festival for allowing the time for its craftspeople to experiment and perfect techniques. The knowledge gained from exploring new ways of creation and realization transferred, of course, to other productions and helped foster a high level of excellence in craft.

The Mikado's enormous kimono, under construction in the Stratford Festival wardrobe, 1982.

COSTUME PAINTER LISA HUGHES, ON WORKING WITH BENSON

"Just a Tidge, Lovey."

I remember a time when we were on the train in a snowstorm returning to Stratford from working all day in Toronto. The storm was so intense the train was stopped for some time while the tracks were cleared. Most people spent the extra time napping or reading, but Susan just kept right on working. A little thing like a snowstorm couldn't stop her and, I think, in many ways this sums up her character: dedicated, hard-working, determined and very, very talented, of course. Susan was many things to me as a teacher and mentor: inspiring, challenging, precise, encouraging, demanding and a perfectionist. We called her "basher" Benson. I'm not exactly sure how the name came about, but it may have been for her combination of toughness, leadership and sensitivity.

Susan always inspired me and everyone else to be creative and innovative. She wouldn't tell us how to do something but allowed us to be creative, all the while pushing the boundaries. She was very generous with a great sense of humour, always giving praise when it was deserved but very serious about the work. Susan helped me to develop "the eye": that indefinable quality that tells you something just works or is perfectly balanced or in harmony. She taught me the importance of spatial relationships and negative space and would often come along to look at something I'd done and ask for — "just a tidge, lovey" — that slight move to the left or right or addition of colour or trim that would make it all come together in a unique, and sometimes surprising, way.

I worked on many shows with Susan over the years at the Stratford Festival and elsewhere, but *The Mikado* in 1982 stands out amongst many rewarding experiences. It was the amazing commitment made by Susan and Brian that carried us all along. No one knew how it was going to turn out, but we had faith in their leadership. Over a long, snowy winter in Stratford, we experimented and gradually worked out the approach that would bring Susan's ideas to life. The Stratford Festival was incredibly supportive and gave us the time we needed to explore new directions, a huge investment on their part. We had Susan's sketches plus research and a general palette of colour for each character but had to work out just how to go about creating the patterns through a combination of dyeing, batik, appliqué and fabric painting. I don't think any of us had an idea, when we started, of how it would turn out. Susan worked with us to translate each sketch into reality and scale the patterns to each actor. For the complex costume for the Mikado himself, she mapped each area out on sheets of brown paper like a giant jigsaw puzzle. We would then work as a team with the cutter to create the approach for each section of this massive costume.

Each costume was different but worked together perfectly as a piece. Susan has an amazing sensitivity to the nuance of colour and would often combine colours in surprising ways. The costume for Pish-Tush, for example, called for many coloured squares of silk, but rather than a repeated colour scheme, Susan would throw in different colours into the pattern to give it life and movement. In contrast to the men's costumes that were strongly patterned, the women's kimonos were softly coloured with subtle patterns that moved beautifully. The overall colour balance for this show was a revelation at the first dress rehearsal. She had worked so closely with the director, Brian Macdonald, to orchestrate each scene through colour; it truly was like watching a moving painting.

Throughout my career as a costume painter, I have worked with a multitude of designers bringing their designs to life on stage. Susan is up there as one of "the greats."

Kimble Hall as Luiz, Eric Donkin as the Duke of Plaza-Toro, Douglas Chamberlain as the Duchess of Plaza-Toro and Deborah Milsom as Casilda in *The Gondoliers*.

CONTINUING THE WORK

Benson's successful collaboration with director Brian Macdonald on Gilbert and Sullivan operettas continued at the Stratford Festival with productions of *The Gondoliers* in 1983 followed by *Iolanthe* a year later. *The Mikado* had set a template for future designs with simple settings enhanced by striking props and costumes. In the same way as the acrobats were used in *The Mikado* to change scenery and props, Benson and Macdonald added Commedia dell'Arte "Zanni" in *The Gondoliers* and stagehands in *Iolanthe* to move the action along and help tell the story visually. The same approach was used in *HMS Pinafore*, produced in 1988 at the Royal Alexandra Theatre, Toronto (remounted at Stratford in 1992). This approach wasn't simply to facilitate scene changes but was intended to include the audience in the humour and theatricality of the performance by creating visual "jokes": a ladder becomes a boat in *The Gondoliers* and packing crates open up to form the British Houses of Parliament in *Iolanthe*. Like much of Benson's work, these productions involved much research and thought to arrive at a seemingly simple, yet visually lavish, production where the focus is on the performers.

THE GONDOLIERS

The tone of *The Gondoliers'* design was set for Benson when Brian Macdonald decided to cast Douglas Chamberlain as the Duchess of Plaza-Toro. This cross-gender casting of a man playing an older woman is a tradition in English pantomime which, in turn, has its roots in the earlier Italian Commedia dell'Arte style. Benson's considerable knowledge and understanding of Commedia, and its evolution into English Pantomime, was essential for this production and influenced every design decision.

One particular challenge with Douglas Chamberlain's casting was makeup. While, at first glance, it may seem this is a type of modern drag performance, the character of the "dame" in English Pantomime has a particular look. Unlike modern drag performance, the typical English Pantomime "dame" is intentionally meant to look like a man dressed as a woman (and a not particularly attractive one at that). No one in the audience is fooled and everyone enjoys being in on the joke. This means the makeup must be crudely done with lipstick that doesn't quite match the lips and with eyebrows artificially arched as if done by a man unused to wearing makeup. Benson initially had trouble communicating this subtle difference and had to correct assumptions about the use of false eyelashes and beautifully made-up eyes that took the humour away from the character.

Benson's colour palette was based on "roses red, roses white," a line from the libretto. This was expanded to a subtle version of the red, white and blue colour theme: red was burnt sienna, white was off-white and blue was a grey-blue. These more subtle tones were chosen as they were in a middle range — neither too bright nor too

Designs for Eric Donkin as the "impoverished" Duke of Plaza-Toro in Act I, and Deborah Milsom as Casilda.

THE GONDOLIERS
Stratford Festival, 1983
Director and Choreographer: Brian Macdonald
Musical Director: Berthold Carrière
Set Designers: Susan Benson and Douglas McLean
Costume Designer: Susan Benson
Lighting Designer: Michael J. Whitfield

dull — and allowed for nuances of character to be expressed through the choice of brighter and darker shades of colour. The production appeared rich, varied and colourful as Benson effectively orchestrated this limited palette. The show began all in white with Commedia figures setting up the stage; colour interest began to build as the female chorus ran onstage. This was followed by the male chorus in blues and reddish browns, then the Duke and Duchess of Plaza-Toro appeared in different shades of blue.

Benson enjoyed designing the costumes for the Duke and Duchess because they had to look broken down and distressed at first then reappeared in all their glory after they came into money in the second act. As the production was very stylized, the first act's costumes were made to appear aged and broken down in a slightly cartoonish way, with texture indicated by painted cross-hatching, stitching in embroidery silk applied to the satin overskirts of the Duchess to represent the repairing of tears, and pieces of old lace applied to the Duke's coat. In the second act, when their finances improved dramatically, the colour range was a jauntier and happier canary yellow with Douglas Chamberlain in outrageous, striped 18th-century panniers.[6] Following the late 18th-century French style of elaborate wigs adorned with all manner of absurd items, Benson designed a sinking galleon in the Duchess' wig for Act One, which became a galleon in full sail for Act Two.

Designs for Douglas Chamberlain as the Duchess of Plaza-Toro in Act II, and two chorus gondolieri. Opposite: Eric Donkin as the Duke of Plaza-Toro and Douglas Chamberlain as the Duchess of Plaza-Toro in Act II from the 1995 revival.

Susan Benson '83

Paul Massel as Giuseppe and John Keane as
Marco with Karen Skidmore as Tessa, Marie
Baron as Gianetta, Glori Gage, Aggie Cekuta,
Marcia Tratt and Karen Wood.

Right: Benson and Brian Macdonald turned
the Act II number "Dance a Cachucha" into
a showstopper by effectively doubling the size
of the cast. A fully costumed life-size doll was
created as a dance partner for everyone in
the cast. The audience didn't realize at first
what was happening because the "couples"
danced on from the wings a few at a time —
eventually filling the stage with a huge crowd
of swirling costumes. At the frenetic climax of
the number, everyone threw their dolls into
the air, then collapsed onto the floor — a true
coup de théâtre.

Opposite: design for Karen Skidmore
as Tessa.

IOLANTHE

For their third successful collaboration at the Stratford Festival, Benson and Macdonald decided to set *Iolanthe* much closer to "home," in Gilbert and Sullivan's 19th-century England. This decision was largely due to the casting of Maureen Forrester as the Fairy Queen; she leant a stately quality to this character, very reminiscent of Queen Victoria. Benson was also inspired by the theatricality and stage effects of Victorian theatre. She enjoyed the fun of swings and obvious stage machinery moving the performers. Her research focused on 19th-century illustrations for the look of the set and the fairies' costumes in particular. She felt the prints and engravings of that era had a romantic quality that was right for the piece.

Benson was happy to be working with Forrester again after her experience on *The Medium*. Forrester was "a real pro" who enjoyed the fun of the production. Even after an unfortunate slip on the set's raked (sloped) stage, she picked herself up and carried on as if nothing had happened.

As Benson and Macdonald wished to keep the same format of lavish costumes and simple, inventive settings as *The Mikado* and *The Gondoliers*, the production began with wooden crates set on a bare stage in front of the brick wall of an old theatre. These crates opened up to reveal a bridge with bullrushes and a river bank in Act One and the British Houses of Parliament in Act Two. The Parliament buildings both unwound and

Maureen Forrester as the Queen of the Fairies, with Allison Grant as Celia, Karen Wood as Babs and Karen Skidmore as Leila. Opposite: design for the Fairies in Act I.

IOLANTHE

Stratford Festival, 1984

Director and Choreographer:
Brian Macdonald

Musical Director:
Berthold Carrière

Set and Costume Designer:
Susan Benson

Lighting Designer:
Michael J. Whitfield

Eric Donkin as the Lord Chancellor and Katharina Megli as Iolanthe; wig and headdress designs, and sketches for the heirarchy of coronets for the Dukes, Marquises, Earls, Viscounts and Barons. Opposite: design for the Fairies in Act II.

concertinaed out to create the building and railings. Actors clad as 19th-century stagehands also moved and pulled larger set pieces onstage and a backdrop and scrim[7] were flown in. For Act Two, when a Palace Guardsman's sentry box was rolled on, Benson worked with a magician to create the illusion of bringing a lot of people out of what appeared to be a very small space. All these decisions were guided by a desire to create a highly theatrical production that encouraged the audience to use their imaginations and join in the fun.

Inspired by British musical hall and variety performances, Benson had fun dressing Marie Baron, who played Phyllis, in an extremely frilly dress and bonnet as she appeared in her first entrance on a swing. In Act One, she created a Victorian version of fairies by dressing them in the frilled bloomers worn by chorus girls at the time, created out of thin layers of gauze. This proved to be a bit of a problem as the real period cut of these garments wasn't flattering. She had the advantage of working with the women in the chorus in two previous productions and, knowing what would make them look good, adjusted the line but still kept the period feel. She also added longer skirts made of layers of transparent material to enhance the romanticism of the second act. In all of this she was grateful to talented cutter, Enid Larson, and her construction team who had a wonderful, light and delicate touch.

Benson enjoyed researching the male chorus as they were required to represent different ranks of the nobility with a variety of crowns and long velvet robes. Working on a raked stage in these long robes proved difficult for some and Benson was grateful for her stage movement training. She was half their size but able to demonstrate how to move elegantly with the trains by wearing the costume herself. At the end of the play, wings had to appear out of the men's court suits. This was masterfully engineered by Stewart Robertson in the prop shop, working closely with the tailors in the wardrobe. It was a magical moment and always made the audience gasp.

CABARET

Working with Brian Macdonald once again, Benson found this production a departure from their previous collaborations. It was the first time they had staged a musical on the Festival's main, thrust stage (an innovation at the time), and the subject matter was much more serious. They saw many contemporary echoes in this story of what went on in Berlin in the 1930s. Benson viewed the musical as a cautionary tale and felt that the design divided into two parts: the world outside the cabaret, which was grittier and grounded in everyday reality; and the theatrical world of the cabaret which, although flashier in palette and texture, had an edge that reflected the shabby, harsh reality of pre-war Germany. To this end, she chose fabric for the costumes that contrasted the escapist world of the cabaret with that of ordinary people. The cabaret costumes, though more flamboyant than the "real" world, were still broken down (distressed) and tawdry.

Although the musical is traditionally performed on a proscenium stage, Benson actually found the Stratford Festival thrust stage worked very well for this production. The strongly architectural space forced her to pare down her vision to the essentials necessary to recreate the world referenced by the musical in the imagination of the audience. The Kit Kat Club, for example, was simply suggested using the Festival's thrust stage as the stage of the club with tables arranged around the edges, allowing actors to view the action from the perspective of the audience.

This spare use of scenic elements was consistent with her approach to set design, and Natalie Rewa, in her book *Scenography in Canada*, points out how this was seen in the production of *Guys and Dolls*, again with Macdonald, on the Festival stage in 1990.[8] This setting consisted of a series of fire escapes constructed in the centre of the theatre's back wall. These were an ideal complement to the stage architecture, providing the feeling of 1950s New York and adding levels for the choreography. The look and atmosphere of each scene was then changed with costumes and props. In both productions, the lighting of Michael J. Whitfield was an essential element to enhance this world and create movement and ambience.

Designs for Brent Carver as the Master of Ceremonies and Sheila McCarthy as Sally Bowles. Opposite: Rosemary Collins as the pianist, Sheila McCarthy as Sally Bowles and Brent Carver as the Master of Ceremonies.

CABARET

Stratford Festival, 1987
Director and Choreographer: Brian Macdonald
Musical Director: Berthold Carrière
Set and Costume Designer: Susan Benson
Lighting Designer: Michael J. Whitfield

Clockwise from top: the ensemble in the Kit Kat Club, designs for Fruit Shop Guests, and Sally Bowles

Opposite: designs for Night Club Guests in Act II.

THE RELAPSE

For this 17th-century comedy, Benson needed to create larger-than-life characters in a period already known for exaggerated styles without creating caricatures. The challenge was to design clothing that was still based in historical reality yet more extreme. She achieved this through the use of strong colours, padding and exaggerated shapes. Additionally, the leading role of Lord Foppington, played by Brian Bedford, had to stand out from the other characters in this world. The character's name is a play on the traditional "fop" character of Restoration comedy — an affected and excessive dandy. For this character, Benson used colours that were not accurate for the period, such as fuchsia, and large black stripes as well as exaggerated shapes. Fortunately, she also had the acting skills of Brian Bedford to complement her work.

An outstanding feature of the production was the wig for Brian Bedford created by Clayton Shields. The issue with all 17th-century wigs is that they must be well structured and not too heavy for the actor to wear. Bedford, in particular, did not like heavy things on his head and so Shields invented a wig made from organza and feathers that perfectly suited the character and the actor's needs.

THE RELAPSE

Stratford Festival,
Avon Theatre, 1989

Director:
Richard Monette

Contributing Director:
Jeannette Lambermont

Consulting Director:
Graham Harley

Costume Designer:
Susan Benson

Set Designer:
Michael Eagan

Lighting Designer:
Michael J. Whitfield

Clockwise from top left: designs for Shirley Douglas as Compliant, Brian Bedford as Lord Foppington, and Paul Boretski as Piss-pot.
Oppostie: Brian Bedford as Lord Foppington, Tim MacDonald as La Verole and David Lloyd-Evans as Cupidon.

THE MARRIAGE OF FIGARO

At their first meeting, Director Colin Graham had envisioned this opera, set in the heat of Spain, with hot colours, terracotta and stuccoed walls, but Benson felt that the music really didn't reflect this mood. To her, the piece strongly evoked 18th-century romanticism and needed a feeling of playfulness, lightness and delicacy. Her research led her to the paintings of Fragonard and Watteau, whom she felt perfectly expressed this feeling. In order to illustrate her point, she worked all night on a quarter-inch scale model to present to Graham the next day, and fortunately he liked her idea.

The libretto of *Figaro* presents a world of deception and intrigue where all is revealed at the end. The first three acts are set in the interior of Count Almaviva's manor, while the final act is in his garden where the truth is revealed. Benson felt this scenic change was significant and her design for the set reflected this feeling of intrigue and gradual revelation by peeling open, then open again with each act, finally revealing the truth in the Count's garden at the end. Each set was placed behind the next so, as the action continued, walls were removed to reveal other walls behind. Eventually all of the walls were removed and the garden revealed. To further enhance the playfulness and romanticism of the piece, the walls of each interior set were painted in the neoclassical style reflective of Fragonard and Watteau. The subject matter of these murals subtly and ironically commented on the action of each scene. The costume palette was very restrained as a counterpoint to the richness and colour of the various settings.

Kathryn Honan-Carter as Cherubino and Tinuke Olafiminah as Susanna. Opposite: Benson's settings for Act I and Act IV.

Janet Michaud as the Countess.

Tinuke Olafimihan as Susanna, Fiona Rose as Marcellina and Charles Andrew Wenner as Dr. Bartolo.

Opposite: design for Valdine Anderson and Janet Michaud as the Countess.

THE MARRIAGE OF FIGARO

Banff Centre, 1990
Director: Colin Graham
Set and Costume Designer: Susan Benson
Lighting Designer: Michael J. Whitfield

Kelly Kaduce as Cio-Cio San, 2014 remount. Opposite: design sketch for this costume.

MADAMA BUTTERFLY

Influenced by their earlier collaboration on *The Mikado*, in 1982, neither Benson nor director Brian Macdonald wanted to emulate traditional approaches to this opera. Benson's empathy for the tragedy of Cio-Cio San led her to create a stark, non-illusionistic setting that didn't romanticize the story. The simplicity of Japanese design fit perfectly with Benson's own aesthetic, as always, putting the focus on the performers. Influenced by traditional Japanese Kabuki staging, she designed a neutral wooden platform as a performance area. This floated, almost like an island, in the centre of the stage, with no curtain, thus removing any fourth wall illusion. Performers entered and exited via two upstage ramps on either side of the platform. Neutrally costumed performers set up large Japanese screens at the beginning of the opera, changed their configuration and moved props with the flow of the action.

Originally Benson staged it for the O'Keefe Centre in Toronto (now the Sony Centre), but she never felt her design quite fit the space. When the new Four Seasons Centre for the Performing Arts in Toronto was planned as a venue for the Canadian Opera Company and the National Ballet, this production was used as an example for the architects of the kind of production the theatre would need to accommodate. As a result, when it was remounted in 2009, it appeared as if it had been intentionally designed for this venue, and both Macdonald and Benson were very happy with the result.

Michael J. Whitfield's lighting was an essential element in creating the various scenes. Benson and Whitfield have a special relationship, and whenever she knows he will be the lighting designer on a production, she intentionally creates a setting that can change with the lighting and the imagination of the audience. In this production, his lighting for the transition from dusk to dawn through the Humming Chorus, while Cio-Cio San faced downstage, was magical.

In contrast to Benson's earlier collaboration with Macdonald on *The Mikado*, the costumes for this production were less decorative. The women's dyed silk kimonos were still long and flowing as they had been for *The Mikado*, but they were more subdued in pattern and colouring. This enabled Benson to use colour to highlight the end of the opera when Cio-Cio San tears off her final white kimono to reveal a raw, red under-kimono. She envisioned this character as a caged butterfly torn apart at the end and pushed to the edge of her world. To increase this effect, the final configuration of screens boxed her into a small downstage area at the edge of the stage.

Brian Macdonald
on *Madama Butterfly*

One of the shows I did with Susan that stands out for me is *Madama Butterfly*. The grey of the new opera house in Toronto and the grey and beechwood colours of the set were absolutely perfect for that production. And Michael Whitfield, of course, creating the lighting.

Over the years of the show, we had different Butterflies all the time as they needed to be young. It's a fierce role as she goes from being 16 years old to a very wise woman, and there's a big range in the singing. The performer needs a lot of heft in her voice but must be slim to wear the costume and Susan was able to adapt to this challenge with each production.

Susan was very on your side as a director. In *Butterfly*, I didn't want an intermission between Acts Two and Three and this caused problems for the design as there was no chance to make wig and costume changes or to move screens on the set. Instead, some of this had to be done in front of the audience, and Susan was very good about this as she knew it helped the flow of the performance not to have the intermission.

Clockwise from top left: designs for Cio-Cio San, Prince Yamadori, Suzuki and Goro. Opposite: design for The Bonze.

MADAMA BUTTERFLY

Canadian Opera Company, 1990
Director: Brian Macdonald
Conductor: Maurizio Arena
Set and Costume Designer: Susan Benson
Lighting Designer: Michael J. Whitfield

Patricia Racette as Cio-Cio San and Elizabeth DeShong as Suzuki, 2014 remount.

Design for giant Lion Mask in the Ballroom scene. Opposite: design for Juliet at the Ball.

116

ROMEO AND JULIET

This was the third time that Susan Benson designed for the National Ballet. Her first production was *L'île Inconnue* in 1983, followed by *The Taming of the Shrew* starring Karen Kain in 1992.

Romeo and Juliet was an exciting opportunity to work with choreographer Reid Anderson who was restaging the late John Cranko's[9] vision of the ballet. Benson was chosen as the designer for her strong background in Shakespeare and her knowledge of the original play. As the intent was to remain true to Cranko's vision, some scenic elements such as a bridge and stairs were essential to accommodate the original choreography, somewhat restricting scenic innovation.

Benson's design was strongly influenced by the darkness of Sergei Prokofiev's music that evoked a dangerous and cruel Verona inhabited by the two young lovers. She felt this archetypal story had been repeated throughout time and echoed a modern case where two young lovers, one Christian, one Muslim, were killed during the conflict in former Yugoslavia. This led her to create a sumptuous, gilded world of shadows and underlying darkness that was true to John Cranko's vision of a corrupt and complex society. Benson's approach surprised and disappointed some critics who expected a more traditional colourful, romantic production.

This innovative interpretation led Benson to design a monochromatic setting which contrasted the opulence in her costume palette and choice of fabrics, enhancing the feeling of a rich, corrupt society with an underlying tone of darkness. Her choice of fabric for the costumes was partly inspired by the need to recreate the luxurious brocades and velvets of 16th-century Verona, but her real motivation was to heighten the emotional effect of the piece by using colour and fabric choices to tell the story.

Romeo and Juliet were in light colours and lightweight fabrics that set them apart from their world, contrasting the fragility of youth with the solidity and power of the ruling and aging establishment. Juliet was like a butterfly let loose amongst this slow, dark, stately court created from decorated velvet. Benson used silk chiffon dyed in gradients of colour for Juliet's dress in contrast to the heavy fabrics of the court, and her character came through in the movement and colour of the fabric. The ballroom scene, where Romeo first meets Juliet, consisted of fiery golds, yellows, oranges and reds set on a black background in order to intensify colours even more. She used metallic fabric and jewellery that glittered in the light to create a night-time ballroom full of fiery potential in this pivotal scene. Like Juliet, the three young men at the ball (Mercutio, Benvolio and Romeo) were set apart from the others with less elaborate clothing, in lighter colours and more youthful in appearance.

ROMEO AND JULIET

National Ballet of Canada, 1995
National Ballet of Finland, 1996
National Ballet of China, 2006
Choreographer: Reid Anderson (after John Cranko)
Set and Costume Designer: Susan Benson
Lighting Designer: Robert Thomson

Artists of the Ballet in the Ballroom scene.

Clockwise from top left: designs for Clowns, a Gypsy, Lady Montague, Tybalt's Ball costume, Guests at the Ball, Romeo and Mercutio.

Clockwise from top left: Aleksandar Antonijevic as Romeo, Christopher Body as Paris and Sonia Rodriguez as Juliet with artists of the Ballet; Etienne Lavigne as Tybalt with artists of the Ballet; Christopher Kiss as Tybalt; artists of the Ballet.

One challenge of the piece for Benson was adapting her knowledge of period costuming to ballet: creating a feeling of 16th-century grandeur in clothing that would work for a dancer. This was particularly challenging in the ball scene, where she used heavy fabrics to create visual weight and opulence. Period accuracy also called for long gowns and trains — all elements that can encumber a dancer. Benson worked very closely with choreographer Reid Anderson to ensure her designs were in concert with his ideas and the dancers' movement. She was careful to bring him to fittings and ensure that rehearsal costumes reflected the final version.

An important element of the setting was a giant lion mask that flew in for the ballroom scene. Benson intended the head to create an ominous feeling as the scene is a turning point in the story. Her design called for a solid centre that was eroding or crumbling away at the edges. Based on older Italian architecture where layers have fallen away over time, the intention was to reflect the erosion of the society of the ballet and the global repetition of this scenario over the centuries. Benson wasn't sure how to best approach its construction until she collaborated with Karen Rodd, who created the masks for the ball scene. As a similar visual impression was required for these masks, Rodd used brass wire to create a metal framework that could be solid in parts and more transparent in others. This then inspired the larger lion mask, which had a solid, carved centre with expanded metal as an understructure. The mask gradually lost its solidity as smaller welded pieces were spaced out from the centre, creating a feeling of erosion.

THE GOLDEN ASS

The Golden Ass is based on Robertson Davies' novel *A Mixture of Frailties*, in which one of the characters composes an opera based on the ancient fable of *The Golden Ass*. This production was difficult to design because Robertson Davies had died in 1995 and was not available for consultation. In addition, the music was still being composed by Randolph Peters in Winnipeg. Since the music is essential in creating a design for an opera, Benson was frustrated at hearing only parts of the opera before her final designs were due. Fortunately, director Colin Graham was very experienced and although not available for much of this period was able to convey his thoughts about the opera's visual world. This still proved to be a frustrating time as Benson felt she was working in the dark creating the opera.

The opera was set in a market town visited by traders from all over Africa passing through its marketplace. The setting for the opera, a series of steps, was like most of her designs: simple yet visually striking with the focus on the performers in costume. Benson's main design inspiration came from the book *Africa Adorned*. This led her to recreate the clothing of ancient Carthage in simple shapes that became the canvas for sumptuous colour and pattern adorned with jewellery and elaborate headdresses. Performers swirled through the action of the opera, changing both the atmosphere and the scene with variations in lighting and costume.

In this production she was supported by a talented team in the Canadian Opera Company wardrobe: costume painters Marjorie Fielding and Lisa Hughes and wardrobe supervisors Carol Holland and Sandra Corazza in particular.

THE GOLDEN ASS

Canadian Opera Company,
World Premiere Production, 1999

Director: Colin Graham

Libretto: Robertson Davies

Composer: Randolph Peters

Conductor: Richard Bradshaw

Set and Costume Designer:
Susan Benson

Lighting Designer:
Michael J. Whitfield

Design for Theodore Baerg as Festus,
the Fabulist. Opposite: design for Judith
Forst as Antiope and prop drawing for
the Fabulist's parasol.

Clockwise from top left: design for a Goddess cape; design for Judith Forst as Pamphilea; Sandra Corazza and Marjory Fielding wearing robes painted by Marjory Fielding and Pam Woodward; Pamphilea's cape in the paint studio; concept sketches for the principal female characters.

Clockwise from top left: Judith Forst as Antiope; Thomas Goerz and Theodore Baerg with Artists of the Canadian Opera Company chorus; preliminary designs for three Goddesses; set model showing setup of screens for Act I.

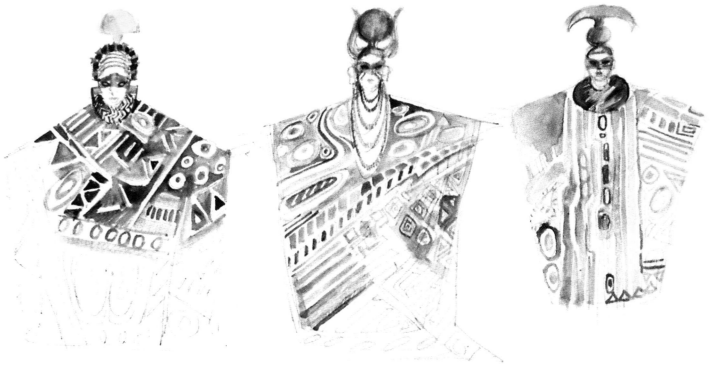

Chronology

1942

Born in Bexley Heath, Kent, United Kingdom

1962

Wolverhampton College of Art: National Diploma of Design

1963

West of England College of Art, Bristol: Art Teacher's Diploma

1963–66

Wardrobe, Royal Shakespeare Company and BBC TV

1966–69

Assistant Costume Designer, Vancouver Playhouse Productions include: *The Ecstasy of Rita Joe*; *Peer Gynt*; *She Stoops to Conquer*; *Androcles and the Lion*; *The Beaux Stratagem*; *Anything Goes*; *Philadelphia, Here I Come*; *A Streetcar Named Desire*

Costume Designer, Vancouver Playhouse, Stage II Productions include: *Listen to the Wind*; *The Miracle Wolf of Gubbio*; *Noh Play*; *Kafka*; *Requiem for a Dinosaur*

Freelance Designer, Vancouver Productions include: *Centralia Incident*; *Pinocchio*; *Under Milkwood*; *Son of Raven, Son of Deer*; *Adventure Story*; *Documents from Hell*; *The Dog and the Stone*; *The Key*; *Luther*

1969–70

Designer, Theatre Centre, Windsor, Ontario

1970–74

Resident Designer for the Krannert Centre for the Performing Arts and Assistant Professor, University of Illinois

1974

The Summoning of Everyman (set & costumes) Stratford Festival, Dir. Michael Bawtree, p. 62

The Medium (set & costumes) Stratford Festival, Dir. Michael Bawtree

The Rivals (costumes) Roundabout Theatre, New York City, Dir. Michael Bawtree

1975

Misalliance (set & costumes) Neptune Theatre, Halifax, Dir. John Wood

The Crucible (set & costumes) Stratford Festival, Dir. John Wood

Twelfth Night (set & costumes) Stratford Festival, Dir. David Jones

1976

John and the Missus (set & costumes) Neptune Theatre, Halifax, Dir. Donald Davis.

A Midsummer Night's Dream (set & costumes) Stratford Festival (with Jessica Tandy as Titania/Hippolyta), Dir. Robin Phillips, p. 66

The Merchant of Venice (set & costumes) Stratford Festival, Dir. Bill Glassco

The Many Faces of Love (costumes for Jessica Tandy), touring show

Harry's Back in Town (costumes) Comus Productions, Toronto

1977

A Midsummer Night's Dream (set & costumes) Stratford Festival (with Maggie Smith as Titania/Hippolyta), Dir. Robin Phillips, p. 66

Back to Beulah (set & costumes) National Arts Centre/Neptune Theatre, Dir. John Wood

The Old Maid and the Thief (set & costumes) Algoma Festival, Dir. David Haber

The Telephone (set & costumes) Algoma Festival, Dir. David Haber

1978

Man of La Mancha (costumes) Theatre New Brunswick, Dir. Malcolm Black

The Father (costumes) National Arts Centre, Ottawa, Dir. Donald Davis

Julius Caesar (set & costumes) Stratford Festival, Dir. John Wood, p. 74

Memoir (set & costumes) National Arts Centre, Ottawa, Dir. John Wood

1979

The Woman (set & costumes) Stratford Festival, Dir. Robin Phillips/Peter Moss/Urjo Kareda, p. 76

Travesties (costumes) Manitoba Theatre Centre, Dir. Eddie Gilbert

William Schwenk and Arthur Who (costumes) National Arts Centre, Ottawa, Dir. John Wood

1980

A Long Day's Journey Into Night (set & costumes) Stratford Festival, Dir. Robin Phillips

A Funny Thing Happened on the Way to the Forum (set & costumes) Toronto Arts Productions, Dir. John Hirsch

Twelfth Night (costumes) Young Peoples' Theatre, Toronto, Dir. John Hirsch

A History of American Film (costumes) National Arts Centre, Ottawa, Dir. John Hirsch

1981

John and the Missus (set & costumes) National Arts Centre/Neptune Theatre, Dir. John Wood

Plenty (costumes) Toronto Arts Productions, Dir. Peter Dews

The Taming of the Shrew (set & costumes) Stratford Festival/CBC TV, Dir. Peter Dews

The Comedy of Errors (set & costumes) Stratford Festival, Dir. Peter Dews

1982

The Merry Wives of Windsor (set & costumes) Stratford Festival/CBC TV, Dir. Robert Beard

Blithe Spirit (set & costumes) National Arts Centre, Ottawa, Dir. Eleanor Fazan

The Wood Demon (costumes) National Arts Centre, Ottawa, Dir. John Wood

1982/83/84

The Mikado (set & costumes) Stratford Festival/CBC TV, Dir. Brian Macdonald, p. 80

1983

Macbeth (set & costumes) Stratford Festival/CBC TV, Dir. Des McAnuff

L'Île Inconnue (costumes) National Ballet of Canada, Choreog. Constantin Patsalus

1983/84

The Gondoliers (set & costumes) Stratford Festival/CBC TV, Dir. Brian Macdonald, p. 91

1984

Death in Venice (costumes) Canadian Opera Company, Toronto, Dir. Lotfi Mansouri

Iolanthe (set & costumes) Stratford Festival/CBC TV, Dir. Brian Macdonald, p. 96

The Importance of Being Earnest (set & costumes) Denver Centre Theatre Company, Dir. John Broome

1985

Private Lives (set & costumes) The Citadel Theatre, Edmonton, Dir. Brian Bedford

Jeanne (set & costumes) Birmingham Repertory Theatre/Kenwright Productions, UK, Dir. Robin Phillips

An Inspector Calls (set & costumes) Grand Theatre, London Ontario, Dir. Derek Goldby

1986

The Mikado (set & costumes) Brian Macdonald Productions, us Tour

Don Quichotte (costumes) New York City Opera, Dir. John Copley

Steps (costumes) Royal Winnipeg Ballet, Choreog. Brian Macdonald

The Heiress (set & costumes) Centre Stage, Toronto, Dir. Eric Steiner

1987

La forza del destino (costumes) Canadian Opera Company/CBC TV, Dir. John Copley

Cabaret (set & costumes) Stratford Festival of Canada, Dir. Brian Macdonald, p. 100

La finta giardiniera (set & costumes) Guelph Spring Festival, Dir. Colin Graham

The Forest (costumes) Centre Stage, Toronto, Dir. Guy Sprung

1988

HMS Pinafore (set & costumes) Royal Alexandra Theatre, and US Tour, Dir. Brian Macdonald

La finta giardiniera (set & costumes) Opera Theatre of St. Louis, Dir. Colin Graham

The Merry Widow (costumes) Mirvish Productions Project, Dir. Brian Macdonald with Cleo Laine and John Dankworth

1989

The Gondoliers (set & costumes) Australian Opera Company, Sydney Opera House, Dir. Brian Macdonald

Les liaisons dangereuses (costumes) Vancouver Playhouse, Dir. Larry Lillo

The Relapse (costumes) Stratford Festival, Dir. Richard Monette, p. 104

1990

Guys and Dolls (set & costumes) Stratford Festival, Dir. Brian Macdonald

Madama Butterfly (set & costumes) Canadian Opera Company, Dir. Brian Macdonald, p. 110

The Marriage of Figaro (set & costumes) Banff Centre, Dir. Colin Graham, p. 106

1991

Cosi fan tutte (set & costumes) Banff Centre, Dir. Colin Graham

1992

The Taming of the Shrew (set & costumes) National Ballet of Canada, Choreog. Cranko/Anderson

The Tempest (set & costumes) Stratford Festival, Dir. David William

HMS Pinafore (set & costumes) Stratford Festival, Dir. Brian Macdonald

1993

The Mikado (set & costumes) Stratford Festival, Dir. Brian Macdonald

Oliver (costumes) The Citadel Theatre, Edmonton, Dir. Robin Phillips

1994

The Pirates of Penzance (set & costumes) Stratford Festival, Dir. Brian Macdonald

1995

Romeo and Juliet (set & costumes) National Ballet of Canada, Choreog. Cranko/Anderson, p. 116

The Merry Wives of Windsor (set & costumes) Stratford Festival, Dir. Richard Monette

The Gondoliers (set & costumes) Stratford Festival, Dir. Brian Macdonald

Season's Greetings (set & costumes) Manitoba Theatre Centre, Dir. Marti Maraden

Prop designs for *The Magic Flute*, Minnesota Opera/Dallas Opera, 1997.

Design for Marie Baron as Phyllis in
Iolanthe, Stratford Festival, 1984.

1996

Romeo and Juliet (set & costumes) National Ballet of Finland, Helsinki, Choreog. Cranko/Anderson, p. 116

A Little Night Music (costumes) Grand Theatre, London, Ontario, Dir. Michael Shamata

A Doll's House (costumes) Guthrie Theatre, Minneapolis, Dir. Michael Langham

Twelfth Night (set & costumes) Atlantic Theatre Festival, Wolfville, Dir. Michael Langham

1997

The Magic Flute (set & costumes) Minnesota Opera/Dallas Opera, Dir. Kelly Robinson

Death in Venice (costumes) San Francisco Opera, Dir. Lotfi Mansouri

1998

Madama Butterfly (set & costumes) Canadian Opera Company, Toronto, Dir. Brian Macdonald

The Mikado (set & costumes) National Arts Centre, Ottawa, Dir. Brian Macdonald

Blessings in Disguise (costumes) Manitoba Theatre Centre, Dir. Robin Phillips

1999

The Golden Ass (set & costumes) Canadian Opera Company, Toronto, Dir. Colin Graham, p. 124

2000/01

The Ballad of Baby Doe (costumes) San Francisco Opera/New York City Opera, Dir. Colin Graham

2001

The Front Page (costumes) Dallas Theater Center, Dir. Richard Hamburger

2002

The Beard of Avon (costumes) CanStage, Toronto, Dir. David Storch

Indian Ink (set & costumes) CanStage, Toronto, Dir. Richard Cottrell

2003

Madama Butterfly (set & costumes) Canadian Opera Company, Dir. Brian Macdonald

2004

Noises Off (costumes) Stratford Festival, Dir. Brian Bedford

2005

Fallen Angels (set & costumes) Stratford Festival, Dir. Brian Bedford

2006

I Am My Own Wife (costumes) National Arts Centre, Ottawa/Canadian Stage, Toronto, Dir. Robin Phillips

Romeo and Juliet (set & costumes) National Ballet of China, p. 116

Gala Opening Four Seasons Centre for the Performing Arts, Canadian Opera Company

2009

Romeo and Juliet (set & costumes) National Ballet of Canada, Toronto

Madama Butterfly (set & costumes) Canadian Opera Company, Toronto

THEATRE DESIGN EXHIBITIONS

1977 Gallery Stratford, *Made Glorious*, exhibition of Stratford Festival costume design

Poster and brochure illustrations for the Toronto Symphony and the Stratford Festival

1981 Gallery Stratford, *A Most Rare Fashion*, exhibition of Stratford Festival costume design

1984 Ontario Crafts Council Gallery, Toronto, *Designing Ladies*

1984 Harbourfront Gallery, Toronto, *Stage Rite*, exhibition of theatre designs

1989 Gallery Stratford, *Susan Benson, Artist/Designer*, Solo Summer Exhibition

1998 Bravo Television, *Originals in Art*

2004 Theatre Museum, Elgin Theatre, Toronto, *Divas of Design: Leading Ladies of Operatic Set and Costume Design*

2008 League of Professional Theatre Women, The New York Public Library for the Performing Arts. *Curtain Call: Celebrating a Century of Women Designing for Live Performance*

For a complete list of Benson's artwork, please refer to her website: susanbensonart.com

ENTRIES IN REFERENCE BOOKS

Canadian Encyclopedia
Who's Who in Canada
Who's Who of Canadian Women
International Who's Who of Women

AWARDS

1979/83/87/91/99 Represented Canada at the Prague Quadrennial

1970 Canada Council Award

1980 Dora Mavor Moore Award, costume design, *Twelfth Night*

1981 Dora Mavor Moore Award, costume design, *A Funny Thing Happened on the Way to the Forum*

1986 Elected to the Royal Canadian Academy of Arts

1986 Dora Mavor Moore Award, costume and set design, *The Mikado*

1987 ACE Award, costume design, Arts and Entertainment Channel, *The Mikado*

1989 Dora Mavor Moore Award, costume and set design, *HMS Pinafore*

1989 Jessie Award, costume design, *Les liaisons dangereuses*

1991 Unsolicited Guthrie Award

1993 The Canada Council Senior Arts Award

1996 Dora Mavor Moore Award, costume design, *A Little Night Music*

1999 Dora Mavor Moore Award, costume design, *The Golden Ass*

2000 Banff Centre Award, contributions to the Arts in Canada

2001 Canadian Institute of Theatre Technology Lifetime Achievement Award

2005 Ontario Arts Council Grant

2009 Honorary Membership in Canadian Actors' Equity for Contributions to Theatre in Canada

2016 Paul D. Fleck Fellowship, Banff Centre

Designs for the Chorus in Don Quichotte, New York City Opera, 1985.

PROFESSIONAL APPOINTMENTS

1970–74 Resident Designer, Krannert Centre for the Performing Arts, Illinois

1981–83 Head of Design, Stratford Festival

1995 Associate Director, Stratford Festival

2004 Member, Inaugural Jury of World Stage Design Exhibition

ACADEMIC APPOINTMENTS

1970–74 Assistant Professor, University of Illinois Theatre Department, Urbana–Champaign

1975/76/98–2006 National Theatre School, Montreal

2007/08 Visiting Lecturer, Costume Design and Drawing, Carnegie Mellon University, Pittsburgh

Guest Lecturer York University, Toronto; Banff School of Fine Arts, Alberta; University of Victoria, British Columbia; University of Alberta; University of Michigan

Workshops American College Theatre Festival, United States Institute for Theatre Technology, Canadian Institute for Theatre Technology, Textile Museum of Canada

END NOTES

INTRODUCTION: A BRIEF BIOGRAPHY

1. The "Doras" are annual Toronto theatre awards, named after the influential Canadian director Dora Mavor Moore, who founded the New Play Society and was vital to the development of Canadian Theatre in the 1950s and 60s.

PART 1: THE MAKING OF A DESIGNER

1. Tanya Moiseiwitsch and Lila De Nobili — both noted female British theatre designers. Moiseiwitsch is known for her work with Sir Tyrone Guthrie at the Stratford Festival in Stratford, Ontario. She is also credited with the unique design of the original Stratford Festival stage.

2. John Bury — noted British Theatre designer who worked for many years at the Royal Shakespeare Company and the National Theatre in London, among many other theatres.

3. This production included a very young Richard Monette in one of the roles. Monette later became artistic director of the Stratford Festival.

PART 2: NOT JUST A PRETTY PICTURE

1. Desmond Heeley — a renowned International designer who first came to the Stratford Festival in 1957 at the invitation of Tanya Moiseiwitsch. Heeley continued his relationship with the Festival throughout his life, made a significant contribution to the high standard of design at the theatre, and inspired innumerable young designers.

2. Michael Langham — British born director Michael Langham succeeded Tyrone Guthrie as artistic director of the Stratford Festival from 1955 to 1967 and continued his association with the theatre for many years afterwards. In addition to *Twelfth Night* at the Atlantic Theatre Festival, Benson also worked with Langham on Ibsen's, *A Doll's House*, at the Guthrie Theatre in Minneapolis in 1996.

PART 3: PUTTING IT ALL TOGETHER

1. The Third Stage, a converted curling rink, was used as an alternative performance space by the Stratford Festival and later renamed, The Tom Patterson Theatre. It is now air conditioned.

PART 4: SELECTED PRODUCTIONS

1. Please refer to the recognition of Natalie Rewa's work in the acknowledgments section.

2. Natalie Rewa, in her book *Scenography in Canada*, makes a similar observation in addition to other interesting comments on this production.

3. Crin (crinoline) – originally made from woven horsehair, is a material often used in period costuming, particularly in hats and headwear. It is made of interwoven material that is light yet relatively stiff and transparent.

4. Rewa, Natalie. *Scenography in Canada: Selected Designers* (Toronto: University of Toronto Press, 2004), p. 150.

5. Kothornoi (Greek pl.:sing. Kothornos) Tall boots with thick soles used by Greek actors to enhance their height. www.whitman.edu/theatre

6. From the French for basket, panniers were basket-like structures that held skirts out at either side of the hips. In the late 18th century, they were said to have reached enormous widths amongst the French aristocracy.

7. Scrim is a versatile woven material used frequently in theatre. When lit from the front, it appears opaque but is transparent when lit from behind. It usually comes in black or white but can also be painted.

8. Rewa, Natalie, *Scenography in Canada: Selected Designers* (Toronto: University of Toronto Press, 2004), p. 148.

9. John Cranko (1927–73) was a South African-born ballet dancer and choreographer, most notably with the Royal Ballet and the Stuttgart Ballet.

ACKNOWLEDGEMENTS

I am indebted to the Ontario Arts Council and Andrew Bailey and Sandra Sabatini at the University of Guelph for their financial support. I would particularly like to thank graphic designers Scott McKowen and Allysha Witt at Punch & Judy Inc. for their care and talent. They have made this a much better book than I could have imagined.

This book would not be possible without the archival collections at the Banff Centre, The Canadian Opera Company, Gallery Stratford, National Ballet of Canada, Stratford Festival, Theatre Museum Canada and the University of Guelph. I would like to acknowledge everyone who gave me so much of their time, support and patience: Angela Brayham, Bev Buckie, Caitlyn Dyer, Liza Giffen, Birthe Jorgenson, Kristin McKinnon, Adrienne Nevile, Jennifer Pugsley, Christine Schindler and Katherine Wilson.

I would like to acknowledge the work of Natalie Rewa, whose book *Scenography in Canada: Selected Designers* covers information on several productions I have discussed. In addition to providing excellent coverage of Susan Benson's work, that book also looks at other important Canadian scenographers.

Thanks to Kathryn Harvey for copy editing and Gavin Semple for reading all of my rough drafts and making corrections. I would also like to thank my research assistant, Sarah Dennison, and Michael Wallace at Theatre Museum Canada for his ongoing support. Thanks also to David Borrowman and Serafina Sebastyan.

I am very grateful to all the people who took time to talk to me, who loaned original sketches, and who were so important in Susan's life and work: Annette Av Paul, Ann Baggley, Dean Bevacqua, Roy Brown, Tessa Buchan, Sandra Corazza, Marjorie Fielding, Louise Guinand, Frank Holte, Lisa Hughes, Brian Macdonald, Joe Mandel, Thom Millest, Susie Proffitt, Dave Rae, Jan Shipway and Gayle Tribick.

This book is for all the designers, craftspeople, technicians and archivists in theatre, whose excellent work is often unrecognized. It is dedicated to Jane and John Benson; to my husband, Keith, for his ongoing support and understanding; and to the memory of Desmond Heeley, Brian Macdonald, Michael Langham, Nicholas Pennell and Robin Phillips.

Sketches of the Court Lady and Court Gentleman from *A Midsummer Night's Dream* on page 70 appear courtesy of the Stratford Festival Archives, Gift of the Douglas E. Schoenherr Collection, Ottawa, 2013, in honour of Robin Phillips, Artistic Director of the Stratford Festival (1975-1980). Sketch of Lord Foppington from *The Relapse* on page 105 appears courtesy of the Stratford Festival Archives, Gift of the Douglas E. Schoenherr Collection, Ottawa, 2018. Sketch of Fruit Shop Guests from the 1987 production of *Cabaret* on page 103 appears courtesy of the Stratford Festival Archives, the Dama Bell Collection. *Romeo and Juliet* photographs courtesy of the National Ballet of Canada.

The Queen of the Fairies' wig and headdress design for *Iolanthe*, Stratford Festival, 1984.

PHOTOGRAPHY CREDITS

Cheryl Bellows 106, 108

David Borrowman 8

Gary Beechey 114–115

David Cooper 96, 98

Michael Cooper 101, 103, 110, 128, 129

Ed Ellis 40–41

Monte Greenshields 107

Lisa Hughes 88

Lydia Pawelak 123 (bottom)

Robert C. Ragsdale 31, 32, 48–49, 58, 59, 64, 65, 67, 68–69, 71, 75, 76, 79, 81, 84, 90, 95, 98, 104

David Street 72, 73, 86

Cylla von Tiedemann 87, 92, 122 (top), 123 (top)

WORKS CITED

Benson, Susan. Interview, 2016.

Motley. *Designing and Making Stage Costumes.* London: Studio Vista, 1964.

Rewa, Natalie. *Scenography in Canada: Selected Designers.* Toronto: University of Toronto Press, 2004.

Shakespeare, William. *Julius Caesar.*

Index